LIVING ON INCOME AT THE AGE OF 40
IN BRAZIL

LIVING ON INCOME
AT THE AGE OF 40

IN BRAZIL

Edition 2010
© Copyright Brazil Real Property 2010
Tutti i diritti riservati

ISBN 978-1- 4467-0475-2
90000

GAROTA DE IPANEMA

Olha que coisa mais linda,
Mais cheia de graça
E ela menina
Que vem que passa
Num doce balanço
Caminho do mar

Moça do corpo dourado
Do sol de ipanema
O seu balançado
E mais que um poema
E a coisa mais linda
Que eu já vi passar

Ah, porque estou tão sozinho
Ah, porque tudo e tão triste
Ah, a beleza que existe
A beleza que não é só minha
Que também passa sozinha

Ah, se ela soubesse
Que quando ela passa
O mundo sorrindo
Se enche de graça
E fica mais lindo
Por causa do amor

Vinicius de Moraes / Antonio Carlos Jobim *(O Maestro)*

IPANEMA GIRL

Look what beautiful
full of grace
she is the girl
that is passing
swaying gently
walking towards the sea

Girl with golden body
by the sun of Impanel
his swing
worth of a poem
is the best thing
I've never seen switch

Ah, why am I so lonely
ah, why everything is so sad
ah, the beauty that exists

The beauty is just not mine
she goes alone

Ah, if she knew
that as she passes
the world smiles
it is filled with grace
and it becomes more beautiful
because of love.

Vinicius de Moraes **/** Antonio Carlos Jobim *(The Master)*

CONTENTS

PREFACE

Globalization promised that, after the collapse of the Soviet Union and the consequent end of the Cold War, a period of Augustan pax, has not failed to disclose the 'umpteenth deception: and the world becomes for a few powerful elites of the board games geopolitical strategy of increasingly pervasive, we are often unaware of the sacrificial pawns in the game.
In this rapidly changing scenario, it is more important than ever to understand where the world is going ... or rather WHERE IN THE WORLD 'BETTER GO!
With this new editorial work we want to reinforce the view, supported by personal experiences, that Brazil is among the few countries still growing in the world and especially one of the last frontiers where you can build a future. Brazil is magic! Paradise is here!
Paradise thanks to its natural beauty, the smile and natural hospitality of the people, good food, to 365 days of sunshine a year, the atmosphere and the feelings that live here.

LIVING ON INCOME AT THE AGE OF 40 IN BRAZIL

With this new practical guide we want to share this magical place together with you.

The paradise exists!

TO RETREAT ONESELF IN BRAZIL AT THE AGE OF 40

Work is the biggest problem that who plan to move to Brazil encounters. We receive daily requests from friends asking if their experience of working in Italy may be useful here in Brazil.

Granted that Brazil is a "continent" with significant economic differences between South and North, and that the majority of Italians want to move to the North-east of Brazil, to the north of Bahia to be clear, that's why work becomes a real problem .. .

Unlike in Italy, North is the least developed area in economy and industry, and lives on mainly by the support of the federal government, by agriculture, cattle breeding and tourism.

Therefore, unless you have experience in these areas, it is very difficult to find a job. In fact the majority of Italians work in the tourist industry (hotels, inns, restaurants, bars, car rental, production or importation of typical food, and then rental, sale and construction of

properties with a tourist destination, etc. ...).

However, there is a whole new way to solve the problem of job.

This one, unlike the other ones, does not require large investments in equipment, but a modest investment in know-how and, as in all activities, such determination, in particular at the beginning.

First things first. First, do not you wake up one morning and decide to blow it to hell and possibly move to the heat on the beach sipping an icy green coconut.

The process is usually long and it is important to dominate it in order not to take hasty decisions.

The phenomenon of downshifting or "reduce the gear" can be the basis of the method to retire before you reach old age and consequently you engage another gear ... the funeral one!

In our case we were approximately 20 years old when we decided that we would have moved somewhere in the tropics in our early thirties.

We advise all those who consider seriously the idea to move to Brazil to learn about downshifting because it can help you to reach your first goal.

In the next chapter we will begin talking about the ways to earn just enough to retire in Brazil thanks to the program of lifestyle simplification now known as downshifting.

DOWNSHIFTING

Downshifting is a social behavior or trend in which individuals live simpler lives to escape from the rat race of obsessive materialism and to reduce the "stress, overtime, and psychological expense that may accompany it." It emphasizes finding an improved balance between leisure and work and focusing life goals on personal fulfillment and relationship building instead of the all-consuming pursuit of economic success.

Downshifting, as a concept, shares many characteristics with Simple living, but is distinguished, as an alternative form, by its focus on moderate change and concentration on an individual comfort level, a "dip your toes in gently"approach. In the 1990s this new form of Simple living began appearing in the mainstream media and has continually grown in popularity among populations living in industrial societies especially the United States, the United Kingdom, and Australia.

Excerpt from the Downshifting Manifesto written by Tracy Smith:

> "Money - We're surrounded by the 'Buy Now, Pay Later' credit culture and have forgotten the value of our true earnings. Curb your debt and prevent overspending by cutting up a [credit] card. **Mantra** - The more money you spend, the longer you need to work to pay for it. **Remember** - The best things in life are free. **Re-learn the value of money and live within your means. Time** - Everybody can claw back time here and there. When you change your perspective on the best ways to spend it, a whole new world opens up. What happened to playing games, reading, talking and interacting as a family? We've just forgotten the joys of doing them all. **Mantra** - What's the point of owning a fortune if you haven't the time to spend it? **Remember** - The most important gift is time. **Spend quality time with the most important people in your life.** "*I hereby pledge to slow my life down a gear, for the benefit of my health, my well being, my environment and for those around me whom I dearly love.*"

Slowing down the pace of life and spending time meaningfully while **not** spending money wastefully are principle values of *downshifting*. Another main tenet is enjoying leisure time in the company of others, especially loved ones, and shunning self-absorption because it resists the normality of individualism and isolation of post-modern society.

The primary motivations for *downshifting* are gaining leisure time, escaping from work-and-spend cycle, and removing the clutter of unnecessary possessions that are accrued while existing in those societies with the highest standards of living and levels of production. The personal goals of *downshifting* are simple: To reach a holistic self-understanding and satisfying meaning in life.

Downshifting successfully demands sustained commitment and trying financial and lifestyle sacrifices. It tests the will and self-control of all adherents, regardless of pre-downshifting economic class. However, because of its personalized nature and emphasis on many minor changes rather than complete lifestyle overhaul, it attracts **downshifters** or participants across the socio-economic spectrum. An intrinsic consequence of *downshifting* is increased time for non-work related activities which, combined with the diverse demographics of *downshifters*, cultivates higher levels of community or civic engagement and social interaction.

The scope of participation is limitless because all members of society, adults, children, businesses, institutions, organizations and governments are able to *downshift*.

In practice, *downshifting* involves a variety of behavioral and lifestyle changes. The majority of these *downshifts* are voluntary choices, but natural, life course events, such as the loss of a job or birth of a child, can prompt *involuntary downshifting*. There is also a temporal dimension because a *downshift* could be either temporary or permanent.

CLASSES OF INCOME IN BRAZIL

The IGBE (Brazilian Institute of Geography and Statistics) divides the Brazilian population in three classes, depending on the income received every month. The upper class (AB) receive an income higher than R$ 4807 (about 2,100 euro), the middle class (C) with an income between R$ 1,115 and R$ 4,807 and the poor class with an income less than R$ 768. The news is that in the past five years, from 2003 to 2008, 25.8 million Brazilians moved to middle class (+ 31%) and about 6 million to upper class (+37%). This means that almost half the population of the 49.22% or 97.1 million Brazilians are members of the middle class and slightly more than 10% of the upper class. 30 million Brazilians remain below the poverty line. Beyond the data, our experience is that Brazil is really experiencing a period of unprecedented growth. The big cities are open-air sites. The crisis only affect tourism housing market because of the crisis in United States and Europe. All this represents a problem for foreign residents but also an opportunity.

A problem because those who think they can live with a pension from Italy see their purchasing power shrink dramatically, other side an opportunity for those who derive their income directly from Brazil or by a business or real estate investment and finance. But one step at a time. First of all let's look how much does it cost to live in Brazil.

MOVE TO BRAZIL

What is expressed below is the result of personal assessments. We tried to be objective and neutral as possible, but nothing can replace personal experience. If you are thinking about Brazil, and you've never been there, take an holiday, in fact, two or three. Brazil is a wonderful country, especially if you can live keeping in touch with inner people and not in the aseptic and baked atmosphere of an organized trip; but the first few days may be too shocking for a European. Not everything is made of palm and bamboo huts on the beach, pink sunsets and starry nights. There are also architectural eyesores, desolate areas, concrete, and other things that sometimes you need to get used to a moment. The fact is that Brazil is poor if compared to our standard of life, and in some ways (sometimes including the architectural and aesthetic tastes) could be similar to our 70s. For example, houses that are normal for the average Brazilian worker or peasant (perhaps houses made of wooden planks or bricks plastered), they appear to us as examples of degradation, and perhaps they are automatically associated with the concept of ill repute; but instead these houses are inhabited by people who have a normal a job, a family, and perhaps people which hospitality is so disarming that we are led to think a bit '...

The fact is that the average Brazilian mentality, for better or for worse, is geared toward a hand to mouth living. "Today I have to eat? Good. Tomorrow we'll see." On one side this means that life in Brazil is generally more spiritual and less material than here, with a tendency to live inventing a way to get by without thinking too much about the future, with a level of stress and competitiveness that we can not reach even on vacation, while on the other side this means that the problem of availability of a serious staff on time to work every day is greater than in Europe, or it means that there are people who remains without food, or even causes the problem make do of children living on the street.

As we said, these are our ratings: questionable, trade unions, to criticism of our result. experience. Consider them for what they are, one point of view, maybe a bit 'out from stereotypes. Use them as you want, but do not take them at face value, just wanted to try to dispel some 'concept pouring out of Brazil that we feel from time to time by people who speak with great conviction about things that have only seen sitting in a chair in front of TV, used to believe in the combination = Reality TV ...

BRAZIL: THE EUROPEAN DREAM

First, dismantle some myths and make some clarifications. Brazil is not a third world country. Who would expect scenes of desolation, poverty, rampant crime, backwardness, laziness, a country bent out of debt, ruled by thieves, dominated by the local mafia, in which one can die for lack of care, you are wrong ...

STEREOTYPES

From a large amount of sample of Italians interviewed, they have not been able to say the names of at least five Brazilian cities, the president of Brazil, or some famous person who was not a football player or a Formula One driver. In addition, approximately 80% of Italians said that males should be on holiday in Brazil (but without the wife or the girlfriend), and that about 90% of women believe that such country is too risky to go on holiday with their children. Asking what are the first things that come to mind about Brazil, most people responded Carnival, Samba, prostitution, slums, crime, gangs of kidnappers who assault people on the street, a fragile economy, degradation, poverty, misery, hunger, etc ...

The majority of interviewed people also believes that universities and schools in general are few and prerogative of the rich, that hospitals in Brazil are few and unreliable, that the language spoken is Spanish. All this suggests, in addition to the fact that most people do not have the **faintest** idea what he's talking about, and is based solely on stereotypes, often spread by the media and tam-tam of urban legends, which tends to unite Brazil with other Latin American states. It does not know that in Brazil there are about 30 million Italians or Italian origin.

Brazil, in many respects, is much more evolved than the average tourist might expect. It 's a country rich in resources, raw materials (the potential of Brazil is scary just to make it a fully independent country, so that could easily survive and prosper without buying anything abroad), dominated by a strong cultural identity and a strong spirit of national unity. Sure, there are differences between one area and another: as half a continent big, it is reasonable to expect. In particular, Brazil is more European, more populous, less wild as far as you travel south. Wild Brazil as we imagine watching documentaries is mainly in the north, Brazil more suited to European lifestyle is in the South. The Sao Paulo state, in particular, could be compared in some ways to Lombardy, and perhaps is the one in which there is a greater concentration of population and the largest concentration of Italian immigrants and their descendants.

SEX TOURISM

Finally, we would like to spend two words about Brazilian women since Brazil has the reputation of the country of easy sex.

Since Brazil is a country where sex has always lived rather freely and with no taboos, women can sometimes be more "friendly" to the Italian / European. But we must also know how to use some discernment. First, the journey from Italy to Brazil does not make you neither more beautiful nor younger. If you are fifty or sixty years old, your wallet being quite swollen, and you managed to find a woman of twenty or thirty years younger than you who smiles and takes you under his arm, you should seriously consider the hypothesis that she is not particularly interested in your appearance or your appeal, unless the reader is George Clooney or Sean Connery.

Now, if you keep your feet on the ground and want some fun it's okay, go ahead, but you have to be such intelligent to figure out what's the aim of the girl in question and don't lie to yourself and to others.

We do not think that a Brazilian twenty years girl can not really fall in love with an Italian who is sixty years old, God forbid, it happens too often, but we are always with our feet on the ground ...

HOW TO START?

Well, let's suppose you have been to Brazil once or twice, and you liked it so much that you want to move there forever. Perhaps you heard few short stories of some friends who sold their house and bought a bar on the beach, or someone who let his home out in Italy and with four or five hundred euros he earns from rent he lives like a king in Brazil. And maybe someone also told you that the way to get a visa to live in Brazil is to go out from Brazil one day a year and then come back (perhaps after you have take a stroll in Argentina,

Chile and Bolivia), and you will have the right to get the visa for another year. Or maybe you just think to be engaged by a friend of yours or to go there and then have a look for a job, or even to sell your car and your bike and start with those ten or twenty thousand euros in your pocket and take over some activity on site. Or simply you are thinking to take your stuff and leave in search of fortune,   product is based on football, sex, samba and beans). Well, sorry, but we're going to bring you back, willy-nilly, with your feet on the ground.

ENTER BRAZIL

1.   You can only go in Brazil with a tourist visa, without preconditions,(as Europeans, the visa will be issued directly to the customs of the airport, after filling out a form that is delivered to you by the hostess on the plane). Tourist visas last for six months (in addition you can request the federal police to give you other 90 days of visa). At the end you have to leave the country and you can not return for six months.

2.   The money you earn from your rent don't let you live like a king Keep in mind that you have to pay to have an health care, you have to buy a house, pay taxes, etc ... so things start to get a bit difficult, it is not advisable to let your home out for rent and go to live in Brazil with your proceeds, unless your home is a castle.

3.   However, you can not just go to Brazil and stop there, unless you want to be illegal and risk being caught and "deported" (Brazilian law uses the very word "deportation").

4.   You cannot request a permanent job-visa to work, unless special cases, for example if your employment status (to prove) is a qualification not found in Brazil; that is, the policy is to give job to Brazilians and not to foreigners. It is not excluded by law, but it is not easy to obtain a visa in these circumstances. So you cannot go and live in Brazil? Of course it's possible, but under certain conditions. Generally you can think about getting a permanent visa, see the chapter "the so-called Residence Permits".

We assume to take a step at a time, and start buying a house in a beautiful rural area, or on the coast, just to get a foothold. How to do it? Well, first get the CPF, which is the Brazilian equivalent of the tax code, more info on the book "Investing in Brazil. What to do and what not to do ... "
The CPF is required for any type of act you do in Brazil, and it's essential. if

you go a step further than just tourism.

The moment you get the CPF and the required documents, it will be easy fast and cheap to buy a property in Brazil in terms of paperwork.

CARS

Buying a car is not a problem, especially if you pay cash. Used cars are more expensive than ours, but this is justified by the fact that new cars cost the same as in Europe, and therefore are very expensive for the average Brazilian, who often must turn to used cars.

However the amount of circulating cars is significantly improved when compared to 15 years ago. Buying a diesel car is not a good value, at least at this moment, it's better to buy a petrol fuel car, which can be easily converted to be fueled with alcohol. It's also better to turn to brands produced locally or at least in South America (eg GM, Fiat, Ford, etc.) because of the low prices of spare parts.

As for the license, you can travel with a driver's license valid in Europe and a translation made by a translator on site, but if you decide to live in Brazil, you have to redo the course and the examination. This is because the translation takes only 6 months and costs a lot. It's very easy, you have to follow a course (6 lessons), to be subjected to a medical examination and an psycho-attitude one, and if you overcome, you also have to follow 15 driving lessons and a practical driving test at the end, which is also rather easy. The cost, in the state of SP, is around 600 Reais ("B" driving license) and around 800 Reais ("A" and "B" driving license). Professional licenses can only be taken one year after completing a successful "B" license.

BANK CURRENT ACCOUNT

Once you have bought a house, and you have power, telephone, water consumption, you can go to the bank to open a Bank current account. You have to Know that probably the bank will refuse to open a current account for a foreigner as you, because is prohibited by law, they say.can not, which is impossible. You must Know that it is not true. Every foreigner in Brazil, under the Brazilian Civil Code, can open a current account; you just have have to find the right branch and it will give you a bank account, credentials to access the account via the Internet, the ATM, your checkbook (Brazil's checks are widely used), and credit card and Visa / Mastercard. In particular, the ATM is very useful as an ATM can do many operations (pay utilities, movements, etc..) without going to the bank office, and it is also essential to make the movements through the internet.

HOW TO DEAL WITH MAINTENANCE COSTS

Most of the utilities consumption bills may be paid by direct debit. With regard to the others, we usually agrees to make a direct remittance to the account of the person or company that takes care of maintenance. Never display yourself as big spenders who do not take care of the costs, or you'll end up paying for things and services more than the real market value, and backtracking becomes difficult.

HOW TO BRING YOUR OWN THING

The first thing that comes to our mind is: how do I bring my things in Brazil? Well, the answer is: you can, but it is not convenient. First of all, to know what you can and what you cannot take, read the rules on the customs clearance of goods:
Import Information:
        http://www.verrua.org/brasile/import%20information.pdf
Also you can also consult the website of Receita Federal, where you can find more information regarding the import of goods but not limited to: www.receita.fazenda.gov.br
As for costs, this is the basic reason why we said that maybe it's not convenient. In fact, the shipment of a 20-foot container (about 33 cubic meters) in Brazil and the of customs clearance and delivery to your home cost approximately of 7000, $ 8,000 or more. In addition, European appliances, which operate with a mains voltage of 220V and a frequency of 50hz, might not work properly with the tension 220v/60 Hz, burning. Instead, the electronic transformers with switching, typically operate with voltages from 100V to 240V at a frequency of 50 Hz to 60 without problems.

After evaluating the possibility to ship their things away, many people are opting to sell everything salable and bring only personal belongings, as well as small items (computer, DVD player, small appliances) that can be packaged and transported as checked baggage or even by hand. In particular, since the electronics are very expensive, you should leave the washing machine and refrigerator, but bring your computer and phone. The furniture can be bought on the spot, is cheaper, and anyway the wood of our furniture could be pleasing to the Brazilian termite, better opt for a local timber and aesthetically more in tune with a tropical climate that is not moving in a dark chestnut walnut.

Pets can be transported by air, sealed in special cages. Find out more at the airline and / or at the travel agency. Many foreigners carry their own dogs preferring direct flights to avoid airports changes and stress to their animals. The transport crates for your pet can be purchased in a common pet-shop.

WHAT DOES IT COST TO LIVE IN BRAZIL

This chapter is dedicated to those who decided to spend the year in Brazil and who are interested in learning more about the cost of living. The tourist visa lets you spend three or six months per year on the Brazilian territory, a period that is quite enough to weigh the pros and cons of this extraordinary country.

Over these past years we have been reading many comments about how much it costs to live in Brazil, and we can assure you that what you will read below is not only written in good faith (you can write something inaccurate even in good faith), but it is documented and verifiable because it comes from our experience.

Life in Brazil is probably more expensive than a tourist passing here the usual two weeks can imagine, but the cost of living here in Brazil and is, of course, not higher than in Europe.

Through this guide we will analyze the costs of housing, energy, telephone, transport, health, entertainment and eating.

We will first take as the reference the "worst" case, the case of a family of four, though this case is rarely, since most foreigners who move here are singles or just live together.

Let's start with two items often complained: education and health (it is advisable for tourists to purchase an Europassistance insurance before leaving for the trip).

In Europe these two items are almost free (up to but what?) but in Brazil they are private, therefore you have to pay for them. This is very true. But of course there is also a public version of both schools and Health (SUS).

HEALTH

The structure of the SUS (public brazilian health) look like those of southern Italy. You don't pay anithing to SUS and you can solve the problem unless it concerns admissions or serious problems. We report this date of fact just to debunk the myth that there is no public health care in Brazil. Of course, to avoid trying your luckis good to do a total health insurance. In Brazil there are several large private insurance companies that provide emergency-assistance throughout the Brazilian territory.
There are two options: the full insurance and the "partnership". The first covers the full cost and the second requires you pay a small contribution at the moment of the performance. The value of the contribution depends on the performance, for example, you pay $ 5R for a specialist check-up against the R $ 80 - R $ 100 that you would pay without the insurance. Our ticket is significantly higher.
This type of insurance, that covers specialist check-up, complex examinations and even hospitalizations, in twin beds costs an average of R $ 561 per month for four people (July 2010)! With about 244 euros a month you have solved the great problem of health for you and your family. Of course there are cheaper insurance, about R $ 300, or more expensive, about R $ 800 (single room hospitalization just like a 5 stars hotel).
We would add an interesting detail: if you had done the insurance alone you would have paid almost the same figure. This is because the value of insurance increases exponentially with the age, so a mate and two young children add approximately R $ 260 to total cost, but they disappear almost entirely because the insurance changes from single to family and you are entitled to a total discount of 2%. This is a real help to the family! The cost of health that we have just quoted is largely compensated by the virtual absence of energy and heating costs if we live in the northeast of Brazil. If you then consider the savings on clothing and footwear (it's always summer) you will also advance money.

SCHOOLS

The question of the school depends on where you live and the establishment you choose. The cost to educate a child of 6 years can range from R $ 200 to R $ 400 a month in a private school. Of course there are public alternatives also in this case. Books and school supplies are from R $ 700 to R $ 1000 a year. If the children are two the value doubles and so on. We can therefore conclude that send two children in a good private school will cost you about R $ 1000 per month all inclusive or R $ 12,000 in a year.

These costs are practically zero when you consider the fact that you will spend no money to go on vacation because you're already there. In fact, how much an average family of four people pay to spend a month for an holiday at sea in Italy? If all goes well no less than 5000 euro or about R $ 12,500. Exactly.

There are still three major items: the house (including condominium, satellite or cable TV, Internet, telephone, water, gas, tax on house), car (including fuel and taxes) and food (including restaurants and beaches).

HOUSE

We have two options: buy or rent, and two more alternative choices for each one: villa or apartment. Obviously, each combination is associated with a different cost.

If you live in a big city the alternative of a villa does not exist but in a city under development, such as Natal, the options are many. Usually cities in Brazil develop from historically urbanized areas with independent houses. The vertical construction expands into these areas through the killing of mostly abandoned houses, sometimes systematic but more often as a patchwork.

Finally it becomes quite impossible to live in a villa in the city, see the case of Salvador, because it is completely surrounded by skyscrapers that remove light and ventilation. Ventilation is very important for those who live in the North-east of Brazil and has a dramatic impact on the costs of running the house. A well ventilated house is healthier and does not need an air conditioning system with all the advantages of economy and health. The difference in cost of electricity can go from R $ 100 R $ 500 per month!

For those who like to live in a single house there is still the solution: the condo of closed homes, or condo Fechado as they say in Brazil. This area is generally located outside the city, closed by a wall, and it provides common facilities, often of high level.

Security, pool, gym, sauna, play area for children, green area for relaxing, socializing area, the inevitable brace or churrascaria to grill or roast meat in the weekend, etc ...

The Brazilians love the "Lazer" or pleasure in the broadest sense ... it's the Latin side of their culture.

An apartment in a building is the only option for those who want to live in the heart of the city and therefore close to all essential services such as schools, hospitals, shopping centers, administrative centers, etc ... As well as condo, homes apartments also have a wide range of services, from the simple ones (24-hour security) to the more sophisticated (swimming pool, sauna, gym, cable TV or satellite TV, internet, churrascaria, a games room, cinema, etc...). All this affect in the cost of condo, that can go from a few hundred to several thousands of R $ per month!

Just consider an Italian condominium: electronic concierge, and cleaning made by an outside company costs about 150R $ per month, but it is almost impossible to find. More often you will find condominiums with some additional service (24 hours concierge, swimming pool, elevator), their cost, depending on the number of owners, can range from R $ 200 to R $ 500 per month for the same services.

In condominiums of homes the same services are generally cheaper because they lack the elevators, maintenance of the building (there are only common parts) and the owners are many.

Electricity costs in Salvador, for example, is R $ 0.44098 per Kwh, plus 25% of taxes. Basically, if you do not use conditioner, do not exceed R $ 50 - R $ 60 per month. It is very common in Brazil to use a device called "chuveiro eletrico". It is an object that is installed in place of the showerhead and instantly heats the water. Energy use is deadly: 4000-5000 Watt, like 10 televisions switched on simultaneously. To be used sparingly. The use of conditioner can rise a lot the bill, so you should buy a good fan, but especially when you rent the apartment be careful it is "lato das ombra", on the shadow side, and it is well ventilated (two windows on opposite sides).

Of course, if you do not buy the apartment yo won't have to worry about paying taxes on house, which are grouped into a single annual tribute in Brazil, called IPTU. The value of this contribution depends on the zone where you live and can be very different.

The purchase price of an apartment or a villa are cheaper than those in Europe, despite the economic crisis and development of the real against the euro have reduced a lot of this difference. Just consider one euro was changed in 2004 to $ 3.7R, while today has been reduced to R $ 2.29 (it's due to the euro crisis and to the development of Brazil with a consequent strengthening of the Real, in simple words "wealth" is shifting from the West to China and Brazil), a devaluation of over 30%! Meanwhile, construction costs have grown by about 7% per year (we are now 5%). This effect is felt mainly on new buildings or as we say here "in lanciamento". The builders have opposed these increases by reducing the square footage of apartments in the same number of rooms. Today a new apartment with three rooms and two bathrooms has an area of just 75 square meters and costs about R $ 250,000. The same apartment but used is purchased about R $ 180,000.

Those who have time and desire will find good opportunities, providing they restructure the building.

The cable TV or satellite TV is available throughout Brazil. In Brazil there is "Cable TV", which greatly reduces the environmental impact (do not see those unsightly dishes). A subscription to the Standard Plus package (Disney Channel, Discovery Kids, Discovery Channel, National Geographic, Fox, Universal, CNN, Space, Warner, and more ...) together with Internet (150KB) costs about R $ 134 per month.

The land line is recommended only for local calls because Skype is the best alternative for overseas calls. They usually prefer to use only mobile phone contract prepaid such TIM, OI, CLARO etc. .. and spend an average of R $ 70 to R $ 100 per month in addition to R $ 50 for Skype (it uses to call landlines or mobiles anywhere in the world as well as Skype users). It's advisable to buy a laptop in Italy because all electronic products are more expensive in Brazil. The cost of a fast internet connection is approximately R $ 50 - R $ 100 per month. Other side you find many Internet cafes. Note: in all the major shopping malls, bars and local bank offices in Brazil there is 'free internet access' and therefore it's normal to see both Brazilians and foreigners drinking a milkshake or a beer while using a laptop or PDA and calling with Skype or other FREE VOIP software.

Taxes on house arrive at beginning of the year into a single municipal tax IPTU said. You can pay a rate, or cash with a substantial discount. Last year, the discount was 30%, this year has been reduced to 20% due to reduced inflation and cost of money. For an house of ours of 110 square meters in the center the value of IPTU was about 850R $ per year (already applied a discount of 20%).

Water and gas cost is traditionally included in the price of the condominium. Some buildings also include other services such as TV, Internet, etc ... Where possible it is better to have an individual meter, at least for water, because the Brazilians do not take care of economy if the cost is commonly divided.

Finally, the fixed costs of the house for a family of 4 with a European standard of living are around R $ 600 - 800. This is quite high because it includes the cost of surveillance 24H (three doormen plus a reserve). The security is the real extra expense that you don't find in Europe. However electronic monitoring system are becoming popular here too, and they significantly reduce these costs.

However, if we consider the difference in purchase price between Europe and Brazil we see that the savings pay this extra due to the need for greater security.

We already analysed the costs of education and health, then those related to house and everything around it.
It remains to analyse the costs of transport and feeding. Remember that even if the costs appear high, they are always well balanced by the savings that occur in other areas.

URBAN TRANSPORT

In many cities the public bus service is widespread and the cost of the ticket is around a real. However, not everywhere there is a single ticket valid for one hour and therefore you risk to pay a real only for one bus stop. The use of the bus is therefore recommended only for long trips, though bumps and sudden braking are on the agenda because of road conditions in the northeast and somewhere else. The watchword is to keep well to the handrails.
There are subscriptions for students and special discounts. For the third age (over 60) urban transport is generally free.

AUTO

You can rent or buy it. We recommend that you rent it only if it's really necessary, and for periods of at least one or two weeks. Dealing with a private you can negotiate a price of R $ 800 - R $ 1000 per month. The alternative is to use the omnibus and taxi when needed. Get a good map of the city, the ones found in the telephone list are excellent, and avoid getting lost in some "favela" in the night.

Regarding the purchase of a car the choice is very wide: now the majority of manufacturers are present with their factories in Brazil, although high-end models are only available for import. Fiat, GM, Volkswagen, Ford, Toyota, Honda, Citroen, Renault, Nissan, Mitsubishi are all present. The cars with 1000cc engines are widespread: Palio, Uno, Fox, Chevrolet Selta, but recently you also find the 1400 and 1600, all engines with strictly FLEX technology (alcohol and petrol).

The growth of the automotive market in Brazil in recent years has been great, thanks to government help (IPI reducida). In Brazil were sold 750,000 FIAT cars in 2009, against 722,000 sold in Italy. This was certainly due to economic crisis over Europe, a crisis that only touched Brazil. Note that the price you pay for the same car with same accessories is more expensive in Brazil than in Europe.

Just take a look at the website of "Quatrorodas" for confirmation. A FIAT UNO FIRE 4P with FLEX engine costs about € 10,000 with no options: no air conditioning, electric locking, electric windows, safety equipment (airbags, abs, etc. ...), radio, CD player, etc. ... Furthermore, the price of use is high, so after the initial devaluation, the resale value remains high, especially for popular models.

Diesel cars are virtually non-existent. Gasoline now costs about 1.1 euro per liter, alcohol 0.83 euro, but you have to consider that alcohol makes 70% of petrol and therefore it costs 1.2 euro per liter. The problem is that cars in Brazil run 10 / 12 km per liter!

For example, a Volkswagen Crossfox 1.6 does 8km per liter! An utilitarian car hardly reaches 14Km per liter: Gone are the 20 km per liter advertised for European cars. On the other hand there are no highways to be paid ... because there are no highways!

The road tax, or IPVA, is equal to 2.5% of the updated value of the car and you pay each year along with the compulsory insurance DPVAT. In this sense it is better than our possession tax because the IPVA decreases as the property becomes older and loses value, while the possession tax remains the same, you would have o pay the same for an old car as for a new one, and forcing the owner to demolition.

Insurance is not mandatory except DPVAT that covers damage to third but for a very limited extent. A decent full insurance (Seguro Unibanco) costs about R $ 1300 a year and obviously depends on the value of the car, as calculated by FIPE. The value of R $ 1,300 is for a car valued at approximately R$ 35. 000.

FEEDING

And finally we come to the cost of food. We will limit ourselves to the products you normally buy at the supermarket.
The food price fluctuations are large enough for the same product and for the many different causes. For example, tomatoes increased from R $ 0.98 to R $ 4 per kg in a few months due to rain, but other products such as milk and extra virgin olive oil decreased in price.
In general, imported products are expensive. Pasta, olive oil and canned Italian tomatoes cost at least twice, three times more than those that are on the shelves of our supermarkets. Thus to avoid mistakes you should refer to a fixed basket of products and use it as a reference. This is what is done for the calculation of inflation. Of course each has its own basket of favorite foods. The choice of food more "Brazilian" such as meat, fish, beans, rice, manioc flour, tomato paste, eggs, papaya, mango and Brazilian pulp, etc ... significantly lowers the cost.
Bread is expensive. The classic sandwich oil costs about R $ 5 per kilo and it is the most consumed by Brazilian families. Also cheese is expensive and low quality: from R $ 30 or more per kilo, except for fresh cheese. Fish and meat are cheap. The prices for fresh fish ranging from R$4-5 ai R$15 per kilogram while fine cuts of meat are in the range of R $ 20 - R $ 30.

The pizza is usually covered with a layer of "Muzzarelli" that has nothing to do with buffalo mozzarella. This layer becomes a very good rubber soles for tennis shoes when cooled, you can find anything on it. The more there are things the more pizza is considered good, and therefore the price goes up. Many pizza stores offer an unlikely cornice (the edge of the pizza) filled with soft cheese (the catupirì), but also with nutella ... etc, which gives the coup de grace to the legendary "pizza margherita" and to client's stomach!
With regard to Brazilian comida, the Bahian is the more tasty eating probably because of the influence of African cuisine. The secret lies in the "tempero", a wise mixture of spices sold in different markets or popular fairs.
The classic "comida a kilo", price per weight, has a cost varying from R $ 10 to R $ 25 per kilo, thus assuming a portion of 600g. and a drink we pay about

R $ 15 - R $ 18. There are also places where you eat for R $ 5 (rice, beans and meat) but we always advise a careful selection of these first.

WHAT 'S THE COST OF LOCAL LIFE?

It is 45% cheaper when considering a European life style. Over the past three years prices have risen by 60%, 30% due to inflation and 30% due to revaluation of the real against the dollar and euro. finally is no longer convenient as before, but you can still live well with a thousand euro per month (note that the minimum wage is 220 euro per month).

LET'S TELL ABOUT ENTERTAINMENT

Brazil lets everyone have fun with a few or a lot of money. An night outside can cost from R $ 15 to R $ 300! The real problem is that here you can have fun all week, unlike in Europe, and therefore also the total budget at the end becomes worrying. Therefore you have to be certain discipline otherwise you will be only one month instead of six.

Enjoy your stay in Brazil!

HOW MUCH YOU SAVE LIVING IN BRAZIL

As already described in part, some of these savings are achieved through simplification of lifestyle or downshifting.
Another part of the savings depends on the climate of Brazil, which provides, especially to those who live in the northeast of the country, a great reduction of energy consumption (15 euro per month for a family of 2 persons) and of the cost of clothing and footwear. In Europe you must have clothes and shoes for four seasons, while in the Northeast there is only one dry season and another rainy season, but with the almost equal temperatures. We can say that if you do not have a mate too vain your expenses for clothing and footwear fell by more than 50%.

Another significant saving is granted by the fact that you will not spend many money to go on holiday at the sea: you are already there. Especially you can go there every day you want. A difficult gain to quantify is the stress reduction and improving health in general. You will see that you begin to feel younger and much more vitalic. Maybe it depends on the sunlight or on the consumption of fresh products with high antioxidant power as Mango and Papaya (fruit, along with bananas, is cheaper: about 50 eurocentsper kilo).

Finally, the lower price of property and a relatively high bank interest allows you to live on income. The concept is simple: sell the property or the properties I own in Europe and purchase at least four times the of properties in Brazil, or in alternative you split your property value between investment in properties and in bank bonds at 6% net.
In later chapters you will find indications about the different kind of investment in property an we will explain the financial details of individual solutions.

MAKE MONEY BY INVESTING In STOCK MARKET OR IN REAL ESTATE?

The recipe to win in Brazil is simple: the ingredients are a capital in euro, for example obtained from the sale of a property in Europe which doubles if converted in local currency, and then the choice of the right mix: real estate / movable investment that best suits your needs.
Most people who decide to make real estate investments for one year think of a profit of "X" percent of the investment. The replacement of the "X" percent varies by country, state, and also the historical moment.

In countries that we call the First World, where financial investments with fixed income that have a ridiculous return for the Brazilians (1% per year, but with inflation close to zero), getting an income around 3% from rent is cause for celebration.

With the monetary stabilization in Brazil, which took place thanks to the Real Plan, inflation and was tamed and maintained at rates that are tolerable so that today is possible to get at least an average return (ROI - Return On Investment) of 9% annual, in case of investments in properties to be rent. Some may contest that there are also investments in the stock market and other financial instruments that allow you to realize greater earnings, except that (especially as shown in recent years) you have high risk of losing your capital in an only one morning, a situation virtually impossible in rent. So in summary, annual incomes from rent higher than 9% have to be considered good investment, while annual incomes from rent lower than 9% have NOT to be considered good investment, in this case you better consider other choices.

Source: Fórum Imobiliário

THE BANCO DO BRASIL IS THE MOST PROFITABLE OF AMERICA

The Banco do Brasil is the most profitable banks in the United States and throughout Latin America.

The average of return on capital is almost 35% and it is not a little thing in these days of bank crisis (many banks have even failed).

Of course in the second and third place there are two other Brazilian banks: Itaú-Unibanco and Bradesco.

PHARMACIES

Another category that lives happily in Brazil are the pharmaceutical industry. After having revealed that the first three banks in the world in terms of profitability are in Brazil (the first one is the Banco do Brasil), we find that the drugs more expensive in the world are in Brazil and in the USA. This is truly the land of the record. The news has an unexpected source, none other than the ANVISA (Agency of Health Surveillance), a government body. In a comparison made with nine nations, Brazil has been exceeded only by the United States, where almost 70% of all drugs for which a patent is still valid are more expensive than in the rest of the planet.

The drugs are cheaper in Australia where, for example, Pegasys, a drug for hepatitis C, a disease that affects 3 million Brazilians, costs R $ 526 against R $ 1,335 in Brazil (116% more expensive).

Fortunately, for many drugs which the license has expired, there are generic drugs whose prices are much more affordable.

We conclude pointing out a fact that's not insignificant. You pay for drugs, in Brazil, even if you pay the health plan. They are free only if consumed in the hospital during the hospitalization.

THE FALSE MYTHS OF BRAZIL

In Brazil, everything was easy. Today, everything is complicated. It's the price you pay when a country tries to stamp out corruption without first having unbureaucratized the state apparatus. If you think that you are not paying taxes you make a big mistake. The IRS is well organized even if it can not monitor all activities. Of course, if they choose to check a Brazilian or a stranger, just think of who will they control... Violence is increasing but is not to critical levels. What is not a myth is the witch-hunt to a certain type of foreign victims they are doing also among people who live and work in dignity in Brazil. Increasingly there are people who end up in the newspaper as monsters and you probably do not deserve it. Lately, even the Italian newspapers have echoed the news coming from Brazil and who is now in this country is accused of sex tourists or pedophiles. Here, however, there are also many Italians who work, who have families and know how things really are. Brazil is not only the one with the red light bar, which basically the same Brazilians made us dream in tourism promotion posters where you could see the bottom of a Brazilian girl on the beach in Copacabana.

WHAT ARE THE MAJOR OBSTACLES TO WHO MOVES IN BRAZIL FOR BUSINESS?

First, the bureaucracy, then the difficulty in obtaining reliable information and professional and skilled workers, expensive costs of launching (certainly not comparable to those in Europe). Then there is the part of the visa and residence, which sometimes becomes a real nightmare. The delays make you live in a state of uncertainty in which it is difficult to invest. Of course, apart from the bureaucracy which is rampant, we can not generalize as regards other inconveniences. There are fundamental differences between big city and the south and the north east and the inner country. Unfortunately, the most beautiful areas of the country that represent the greatest interest to small investors are the most disadvantaged.

37.5% PROFIT

In January 2010 we published our book "INVESTING IN BRAZIL! WHAT TO DO AND WHAT NOT TO DO ... ", revised edition 2010, the following is an excerpt from the chapter" Why 'Brazil' with 5 good reasons:

1) you do not leave anything behind you, only problems and an uncertain future ...

2) the change will not be more in favour in the future. The maximum value reached during the first election of Lula was 1 euro changed to 4 , but all of Latin America seemed on the verge of bankruptcy. Argentina had just failed, in Venezuela there was the golpe that deposed President Chavez and Brazil, for the first time it seemed that the eternal second Luiz Inacio Lula da Silva of the feared Workers' Party could take the power.

Things have gone then as we know: Argentina has renegotiated its debt, Chavez went back triumphantly in Caracas and was re-elected, Lula became really the new president of Brazil but, against the fears of economists, Brazil grew as never before. under his government. He was certainly lucky because, thanks to market opening to China, there has been a huge demand for raw material of which Brazil is the main exporter: soy, iron ore, orange juice, coffee, sugar.

3) The cost of living is still relatively low. You live quietly with 1000 euro per month, and you will not spend money to go to the sea on holiday because you already are there.

4) The interest on Treasury Bill in Brazil, although they have decreased substantially, they are now at 10% net.

5) The climate is excellent (at least in the northeast) which results in a drastic reduction in costs for heating and clothing. Bermuda shorts, polo shirts and flip-flops all year round! And the Brazilians are friendly and helpful. The average age in Brazil is 28 years, and do not forget the music, excellent food etc ....

Well, reading again we think we made a really good service to those who, after they had read, they followed it. Considering that at the time of the book the exchange rate was 1 to 3 (1 euro is equivalent to 3 reais), who had invested € 200,000 would find itself with an equivalent value of 260,000, only because of the change (now change is equal to 1 : 2.3, one euro is equivalent to 2.3 reais), and then with 286,000 euro if, following another suggestion in the book, had also invested in Treasury Bill in Brazil.

IT'S BLACK CRISIS!

Germany, allied to the United States and China, is trying to use its dominant position in Europe to take not only the monetary sovereignty but also the political sovereignty of the countries that have debt problems. The excuse is that they want to maintain the healthy balance sheets. In reality we know that the U.S. are in a worse mess than some European countries, and that the Germans have their welfare because of their dominant position in the euro area, as well as the monstrous interests that German banks earn from the sovereign debt of PIIGS countries - Portugal, Ireland, Italy, Greece, Spain who must undergo SLAVERY to pay such interest !
The Americans exploit the weakness of the euro in order to attract capital, their last big chance, to get rid of dollars to the Chinese, before the final collapse of the U.S. dollar.
Those who can not have healthy balance sheets to avoid leaving the euro area must cede control of political decisions to Europe. On this basis, Europe does not exist and must not exist. But if no one complains, the player who raises his voice gets what he wants.

But in reality, Germany has everything to lose by default in Greece or other countries, as German banks hold 520 billion of securities of PIIGS countries. The default of PIIGS country is equivalent to default of Germany. So if the Greeks accept passively the will of the Germans they would be lost. But if they fight and make a popular revolt, they will force the Germans to run for cover. This is a war and the best strategy will get huge benefits. Why should a nation lose its sovereignty? what are the benefits of a Germanic Europe? What would Germany make with Greek people? Simple: would command, require sacrifices, require its companies, its products ... and would hardly help the economy and the spirit of individual liberty. United Europe is not like Germanic Europe.
It would be better for Greece not to pay the debt ... as many homeowners did with sub-prime debt ... rather than living as slaves to debt and being unable to pay it back ... ... they took the keys and gave back a no value house to the banks ... bringing down the system.
The Greeks would go maybe 60 years back? What the hell is the problem? Retrieve the desire to roll up their sleeves, the desire to grow and create the basis for their own dignity. There could be the space to revive the concept of true democracy and autonomy of monetary policy.
Of course, the sacrifices would be the biggest, but often the winning choices are the most uncomfortable. Also because they give in to blackmail very heavy, with a lot of unknowns about the future.
But unfortunately it's already known that the Greeks have passively accepted

the will of the Germans, or rather, the Fed and the ECB, and then they are lost.
Portugal, Ireland, Italy, Spain and several Eastern European countries are on the same road ... ... (Just a bit late, as they have a little more private savings and a bit more of manufacturing bases, but the accumulated debt and non recovery leads to the same critical state experienced by the Greeks).

THE SOLUTION COULD BE:

1) Creditors (who have committed a gamble when they lent money) must accept a renegotiation of the debt (getting satisfied with 70% of what they invested) as holders of Argentine bonds made. That is in fact the same principle.
2) Europe must emit a single debt, and the funds collected should be divided equally between countries linking them to the default settings and not subject to German control. At that point no assistance to Greece to be asked individual European countries ... (Avoiding that individual PIIGS countries should increase the suffering sovereign debt rate differential with Germany, accelerating the process of their race to the abyss).
3) The greek people only at that point will have to accept sacrifices (sacrifices must be equally divided ... also the banks must pay, and if they can not pay, they have to be nationalized or should fail ... as it would have gone in March 2009).

Unfortunately, this was not and the Greeks passively accepted the will of the Germans, or rather, of the Fed and the ECB.
So now PIIGS should rise up together and put under pressure (blackmail) the Germans ... then their economy would be the one more at risk, as Germany would be put into a corner.
Just as the Americans do with the big Chinese lenders. The debtor, not the creditor, makes the rules. they can do this because the fortunes of China (for now) is linked to U.S. debt.
Germany, discrediting one small country, is playing in a strong position of blackmail against other debtors in the periphery.
But if all peripheral debtors (PIIGS) link together ... Germany (or rather who is behind them) should give up.
Debtors have a duty to unite and rebel ... throwing panic into the arms of the Germans   ...   who   would   see   their   banks   value   fall   by   80%.
Unfortunately, governors of PIIGS are divided among themselves and unable

to link together, and the result is financial maneuvers by those countries that suppose sacrifices in "blood and tears," maneuvers that do nothing but buy time by returning default.

NEW RECORDS FOR THE UNEMPLOYMENT RATE IN EUROPE

Data on unemployment levels get worse in the EU. The rate for the euro zone countries reached almost 9.6%, while for the 27 Member States it stands at 9.1%

No good news come from Eurostat on the job market in Europe. The European Statistical Office has just released data reported in August, registering an unemployment rate of 9.6%, the highest level ever recorded since March 1999. Things are no better for the 27 EU Member States: 9.1 percent, the highest recorded since March 2004. The latest data from Eurostat confirmed the negative trend highlighted in recent months. The unemployment rate in July in the euro area stood at 9.5%, slightly below the 9.6 percentage points in August just past. In the same period of 2008, it was around 7.6%, reflecting the strong influence of the crisis on the job market over the last year. The level of unemployment in the EU 27 was 7.0% in August 2008, against the current 9.1 percentage points.

According to the European statistical office, in August just passed the total number of unemployed stood at 21.872 million share in Europe, of which 15.165 million in the eurozone itself. In just one month, the number of unemployed has risen by well 236,000 units in the EU 27 and 165,000 units in the countries of the Euro. The figure reveals the worst course in a broader perspective than in 2008, the total number of unemployed has increased by more than 5 million, with a peak equal to approximately 3.2 million in the eurozone.

A trend that confirms the many concerns raised in recent months about the possible getting worse of the conditions of the job market on the continent because of the crisis. The worst data belongs to Spain, which recorded an unemployment rate of 18.9%. The other major areas of pain on the face of unemployment were taken by Eurostat in Latvia and Estonia, countries in which the number of unemployed has increased respectively from 7.4% to 18.3% and from 4.1% to 13.3 % in just one year. Sensitive on-year increases in Germany, from 7.2% to 7.7%, and Belgium, from 7.5% to 7.9%. The trend in the unemployment rate less punishing some states like the

Netherlands and Austria, respectively, still at 3.5% and 4.7%. The number of unemployed remained essentially stable in Italy to 7.4% (as of June 2009) compared to 6.8% recorded in August of 2008, but the performance of the "Bel Paese" in employment can not be compared with recent data for other European countries due to the quarterly survey data.

In addition to detail on individual countries, Eurostat has also published some interesting analysis on the composition of the pool of unemployed in Europe. The unemployment rate for men rose in a year from 7.0% to 9.4% in the Eurozone and from 6.7% to 9.1% in the 27 Member States. Less pronounced trend for women, whose unemployment rate was already higher than that of men: 8, 3% to 9.8% in the Eurozone and from 7.5% to 9.0% in of the 27, again on an annual basis. Finally, the unemployment rate among under 25 recorded during August 2009 amounted to 19.7 percent in the eurozone and by 19.8% in the 27 Member States. A year ago these figures were respectively equal to 15, and 15.5 percentage points.

The level of unemployment in Europe has therefore assumed levels comparable with U.S. data. According to the latest figures, in fact, the U.S. unemployment rate reached 9.7% share during the month of August. In this situation, living abroad, especially in Brazil, is a good and safe way of life.

THE PYRAMID OF NEEDS BY MASLOW

What are the reasons that lead an individual to work? Abraham Maslow, in the '50s, developed a theory called "ladder of needs" or "pyramid of needs". It is assumed that, once an individual perceives a need, puts in place the tools best suited to meet it.

According to this theory, the perceived needs of the individual are grouped into five different categories and are organized with a clear hierarchy, for which a need is not motivating an individual if he has not first satisfied the needs in the lower level of the hierarchy.

At the base of the pyramid there are physiological needs, related to the very survival of human beings (hunger, thirst, rest, shelter). These needs are the first that must be met and, just as they are satisfied on a regular basis, there are other needs in the individual level.

Then we find the security needs, to be intended as physical security, guaranteed by rules that protect health and safety of workers, as a need for job stability, and assistance in case of unemployment, disease and injury. Essentially, we have needs related to the desire for protection and peace of mind.

A step above in the scale of needs, there are social ones, or a sense of belonging to the group, the need to be accepted by others, to receive friendship and affection. Then there are the esteem needs to be understood in the sense of esteem of others that self-esteem.

On the top level of the pyramid there are the needs of self, which consist in wanting to be what you want, according to one's abilities and aspirations and determination to be in a satisfying position in the group. According to Maslow, a need not regularly met has a high motivating force. In addition, a need is not motivating if the needs of lower hierarchical level have not been fulfilled, so in order that a need for higher ranking emerges is necessary that those of lower order have all been met.

In the more economically advanced society, where the needs of lower level of the hierarchy are commonly met (such as physiological needs as well as security), the motivation for self esteem and take precedence over other needs hierarchically inferior.

Maslow's pyramid has been the subject of some criticism, for example:
- not necessarily have to go through all levels of the hierarchy, while it is possible that some of them are skipped. In fact, individuals may perceive needs differently, so some may choose to meet the needs of higher degree sacrificing other lower order;
- scales of individual needs can be different in different situations and different economic and cultural environments;
- the theory excludes that an individual may be driven by more than one need at the same time, with different intensities.

WORKING IN HARMONY WITH LIFE

the importance of working happily and cheaply emerges by ISPESL research on the physical and mental health of workers,

Work-related stress affects 22 percent of workers. Studies conducted by ISPESL, National Institute for Occupational Safety and Prevention, showed that a percentage between 50% and 60% of working days lost is just due to stress, which involves a 22 million euro of employment a year because of work-related stress.

The causes of work-related disorders can be manifold, including the introduction of new technologies rather than new flexible forms of contract, type of profession and organization of the work context. Psychological and psychiatric disorders on the rise, linked to the adaptation or of anxiety-depression are often related to work situations unnerving, affecting in particular subjects ranging between 35-44 years.

As we have already pointed out on another occasion, it is essential to convey to employers the importance of creating a healthy environment, free from anxiety, in order to obtain not only a corporate savings, but also the welfare of the workforce . Stress and conflict at work, which is exacerbated in times of trouble, most hinder the management of a crisis.

According to the British National Institute for Health and Clinical Excellence (NICE), a responsibility to address the spread of these diseases must be investigated in the figure of managers and executives, who should revisit rigid and authoritarian attitudes in order to leave more space in the positive feedback respect of subordinates, giving greater freedom and autonomy by increasing self-esteem and autonomy at work.

According to the European Campaign on Mental Health, "Working in harmony with the life", you must:

understand and prevent the factors leading to stress and mental health problems;

offer support to employees who have mental health problems; develop corporate policies for the rehabilitation and / or use of those with mental health problems.

Even legally, the term "health" has been expanded significantly, indicating not only the absence of disease or infirmity, but also a state of physical, mental and social well-being, introducing as a risk factor for work-related stress. The mental and physical health of staff, becomes an essential point.

BURNOUT

Burnout is the "do not do it anymore", the dissatisfaction and daily irritation, prostration and emptying, a sense of disappointment and helplessness of many workers.

Some identify it with the stress of working, specifically in the helping professions, but the attitude of indifference, cynicism and ill will towards the recipients of one's work make it a contagious virus of the soul, subtle, invisible, penetrating.

To address the problem is therefore advisable to adopt a preventive approach. The current working environment, shaped by social forces, cultural and economic risk might be put to the test organizations, forced to increase productivity, to re-engineer operations and to resist opportunistic exploitation. And the workers? Internalize these changes and turn them into physical and psychological stress.

So it becomes a burnout stress syndrome no longer exclusive of helping professions, but probably ill-managed in any organization, where you work with no organization and poor and inadequate remuneration.

WHAT "STORIES" DO YOU TELL YOURSELF?

Change your life? Arduous undertaking. Open a business without capital? Too risky.

Did you ever give up an important goal only because you believed that you could not make it happen? You're not up to do it? According to Anthony Robbins, the motivational trainer and coach of the world's No. 1 world leaders like Bill Clinton and Donald Trump, "beliefs" influence our actions and therefore determine our results.

What are the beliefs? Are the set of thoughts and ideas embedded within us, those beliefs we have about ourselves and relationships with others, are the maps that guide our actions and affect our way of being and acting. Consider the beliefs that may limit our attitudes. If a boy is believed to be a poor student, how this belief will affect its performance at school? he probably do not promise more than is necessary, because he is convinced he could not improve his level.

The good news is that beliefs are a choice! What you are is what you choose to be. The way you live is what you choose to live. You have the power to change reality if you just learn to focus on the beliefs that will enhance, rather than those that limit you.

This does not mean that a strong conviction is enough to get results: work on one's beliefs is a process that requires commitment and perseverance. Here then three "sources" to be drawn on to develop empowering beliefs: 1. Environment. "Few people are able to express views different from their own prejudices coming from their social environment." Albert Einstein. Our brain is a sponge that absorbs unconsciously everything that happens around us. Beliefs, attitudes of those around us inevitably influence our own. Search therefore people who can influence you positively, that you estimates for the results they have achieved and can be a model for you. Immerse yourself in their environment and make it yours!

2. Experience. Experience is the foundation of our beliefs, because it is through this that we develop the vision of ourselves and others. Create opportunities for new experiences, meet new realities, new people. You can go to cinema more often, read a newspaper every day, attend training courses. The more tou walk out from the limiting and drawings that influenced you, the more you get knowledge and thus you build new beliefs.
3. View future experiences. As past experiences affect our actions, the same is true if every day we focus our future. View the realization of what we set for ourselves can considerably empower our beliefs. Think of a sales target for this year: it is easier to earn € 10,000 or € 50,000? If you think it is easier to earn 10,000 euro you tend to limit yourself. Involving the money to the effort will adversely affect your performance, creating you anxieties and frustrations at work and going to undermine your results. Conversely, if you think it's easier to earn € 50,000, you know you have the right tools to accomplish your goal statement. Probably you associate money with the welfare and you like to imagine what you could do after you have achieved your goal: buy a bigger house, go on holiday with your family, have more time for yourself. These views will be the fuel that will push you every day to work harder and better to achieve your goals. Remember: what you decide to build inside and outside of you, will be your future .. just because you have the power to choose who to be and to live the way you want. For more about these issues suggest reading the book worldwide bestseller Anthony Robbins "How to improve your mental, physical, financial."

MISTAKES YOU LEARN: THE VALUE OF FAILURE

A famous proverb says: "Practice makes you learn." It might seem like a comforting phrase, as if to say "Do not turn the knife. We do not make the person who made a mistake feel guilty for it, more than what is necessary. " But in reality it is true: the failure can be a useful opportunity for growth and learning. Often we imagine that we are faced with a goal in the sphere of personal or professional, we can take two different paths:one is a string of successes, and one of only scattered failures and mistakes. But the reality is never like that and we must overcome a number of obstacles and difficulties to be successful. And that we can reach the goal fixed in advance only by addressing and overcoming these difficulties. As Thomas Vince Lombardi says, a football coach, "the most successful is not to never fall, but rise again after every fall." Avoiding mistakes is so rather unlikely, but they can be transformed into constructive moments that help you to grow and allow you to do one more step toward the goal fixed in advance. For this to be possible we must avoid placing ourselves in front of the error with an attitude of self-pity and a sense of guilt and pessimism or looking for a scapegoat. The error, the chance to often miss are enough to scare, and will even be able to stop any decision or action: it's better doing nothing than doing something wrong. "To err is human", says another proverb, therefore, do not be afraid of the possible errors . It is the failure indeed, that brings about change and desire to tread new paths. We must learn from our mistakes so we can make new strengths from them. But why a failure can not be considered as a bad thing? First, as mentioned above, every error can be a time of learning. A small child learning to walk fell many times and each time gets up. From experience, even negative,we learn and acquire the capacity not to repeat the error in similar situations. The failure increases the maturity, can make it stronger than what happens when everything goes your way, increases the ability to get out of difficult situations. When we fail, we stop and ask ourselves if we're on the right track, what we did wrong, how can we avoid the same mistakes, what we have to change. And why not, failure can give us the strength to leave the old road to travel to new ones and may be so, a significant source of new opportunities.

JOB SATISFACTION

The term job satisfaction is used for the first time in 1935 by Hoppock. Over the years many theories have occurred and many researches were directed to understand what factors determine the job satisfaction The word "work" indicates the use of energy for a specific purpose, but in colloquial language is also used to indicate fatigue, stress. No coincidence that the work is often associated with dissatisfaction or stress. According to Taylor workers are persuaded to work for their particular interest in the money, with the result that a satisfactory job situation is represented for them by the entitlement to receive a decent wage with minimum effort. In 1927, Henri de Man said in his text (The joy of work) that the understanding by the worker of the social utility of his work can increase his satisfaction. Between

1927 and 1932, Elton Mayo and his team of researchers conducted a series of experiments in order to highlight relationships between such factors as number of hours worked, frequency and duration of rest breaks and work performance. These experiments show a steady increase in yields, but without any precise relationship to the factors examined. The hypothesis advanced by Mayo is that the yield improvement is due to the increased satisfaction of workers to be monitored. In 1935, R. Hoppock used for the first time the expression satisfaction *job*. He, as well as building an index to measure overall satisfaction, says the job satisfaction which can not be considered separately from the general satisfaction in life. The satisfaction for the work of an individual may depend on many factors:
- content of the work, such as tasks, methods of carrying out the tasks, physical environment in which the work is done. According to Hackman and Oldham (1976) complex jobs are generally more satisfactory than the more repetitive;
- organizational climate, such as reports that are created with other workers, with higher support from them, cohesion among colleagues, the standards applied in the workplace, formal organization, innovation, work pressures, etc. .. Mayo (1949) states that "the desire to be esteemed by their peers, the so-called instinct of association, is far larger than the narrow self-interest";
- economic factors. Regarding the link between job satisfaction and retribution not all the studies reach the same conclusions. According to Lawler (1971) wages satisfaction depends not only on how much the employee receives, but also by the perception of what he should receives and from the perception of what others receive;
- other personal factors such as personality, age, educational level, cultural environment of origin. Thus, for example, within the growing of economic and professional level, people generally feel more strongly the need for esteem and self-realization.
It should however be noted that these factors are not equally important in all subjects: some of them may be more prevalent for some workers, but could be of less importance for others.

THE TYPICAL SPEECH OF THE SLAVE

One of the most deadly sides of the culture, is to believe it's the only culture
... but it is simply the worst.

Well, the examples are in everyone's heart ... for example the fact that people
go to work six days a week is the most beggarly you can imagine.
How do you steal the lives of human beings in exchange for food, bed, little
car...

While until yesterday I believed that it had been a pleasure to give me a job,
now I think:
"look how these bastards are stealing the only life I have, because I will not
have another
I've got this ... and they just make me go to work five, ... six days a week and
leave me a miserable day ... what for? How can you build a life in such only
one day? "

So while one should not put the flowers on the window of the cell of which he
is a prisoner,
because otherwise if one day the door will be open to him he will not quit ...

he should always be thinking, with a perfect consciousness:
"They're stealing lives, in exchange for a thousand and four hundred euro a
month, at best, while I am a work of art whose value is unspeakable"

I do not understand why a painting by Van Gogh is 77 billion worth while a
human being is a thousand and four hundred euro worth a month, if it goes
well.
In my opinion, then, since there is a parameter that, with new technologies,
profits have increased by at least 100 times ... and then the work had
decreased by at least 10 times! But no! The working time has remained
intact. Today I know that they are stealing the most precious thing I have
been given by Nature. Think about the best thing that nature offers, which is
to, say, make love, not!

Imagine that you live in a political system, economic and social, where people
are obliged to make love eight hours a day ... would be a real torture ... so
why should not be the same for the work that is certainly less pleasant than
making love, or not?! For example, the fact that people go to work six days a
week ... of course I've got the gun to the head ... I do, because I do the

46

speech: "it's better to lick the floor or to die?"
"Better to lick the floor" but what is horrible in this culture is that "lick the floor"
has actually become an aspiration, you know?

But it is monstrous that he has to go to work 8 hours a day and should be
grateful to the one who make him lick the floor, you know?
Everything is "objectively" monstrous, but where consciousness produces
consciousness, everything is "actually" Monster ...

"Okay, But now the SITUATION is irreversible"

Yes, you make such a speech in defense of those who oppress you, because
it is typical of the slave, or not! The true slave ... the himrue slave defends
master, does not fight him. Because the slave is not really the one who has
the chain to the foot, but who is no longer able to imagine himself free.

But about what you told me now: when Galileo stated that the Earth revolves
around the Sun, there was certainly someone like you, who said:
"Oh yes! In the last 22 centuries everyone says that the Sun revolves around
Earth, and now you come to say this shit ... and how will you explain it to all
human beings?" And he said: "It's not my business, gentlemen ..."

"So look, we will meanwhile lower you into a well unless you say that it is not
true, so all things come back in order" ... do you understand? Because all the
West live in an area of benefit because it is stealing 8 / 10 of the assets of the
rest of the world. So it's not true that we are living in a political system
capable of giving us television, the car ... no.

It is a political system that knows how to steal 8 / 10 to 3 / 4 of the World and
give a bit well-being at 1 / 4 of the World, us ...
then, gentlemen, wake you up ... or you pretend to sleep ... or do you realize
that you are all dead ...

Silvano Agosti

LIFE OF INCOME

Why not, and, above all, without being ashamed of being considered lazy. It 's not the most desirable job in the world.

It is important to be clear that you can change residence and profession from one day to another, but a way of life can not be improvised. The turn should be weighted, measured, and, above all, planned. Decided so quiet by the rest of the family, if you are not alone.

For the West, think of the decline is not only inevitable. It's desirable, since it is the only non-confrontational and non-destructive way to go towards a more relaxed, deep and supportive society, serene, in a word.

Use an income to live can seem like a dream for a few. In fact, to power the determinants of happiness there is not only the purely economic aspect. Is it not a crime to think, at a certain stage of life, to distort the classical paradigm subsistence=income, and to evaluate alternatives to fulfill the slumbering possibility of being able to finally take up the pursuit of one's ambitions without producing the longing alternatives earnings.

In fact, most advanced societies are dynamically leading to the pursuit of income "on the person" as a principle of existence thanks to its continued aging. In Northern Europe it is common practice devoting to not income-centric jobs (hobbies, travel, social commitment). Thinking that income must come from a balance sheet feeding is not always true, in the right perspective of reviewing the new opportunities, it follows an acceptable overall balance while living slightly below your means, but giving emphasis to intangible aspects such as welfare , serenity, satisfaction, social, life returns to the center of gravity and the personal ROI (return on investment) may be reconsidered in a new light.

The drastic slowdown of the economy focuses on the need to diversify the commitments in our lives, such to fill potential "dead time" forced by sluggish working employment, as well as having to think of a better redistribution of resources to ensure a future which is "like never before ..." .

So here come forward new terms on which will upgrade the quality of life:
- Degree of perceived control of one's present and future life as the ability to be able to decide on oneself and the sense of independence that it yields: proactivity towards what currently affects us: surely time is still scarce and a not compliant income can often put into question, giving priority to commitments implies a forced choice recognized as a loss of control over their lives.
- Participatory and relational commitment as an exercise, and then sharing the raising of achievement of social objectives of congenital pure spirit of human nature (the success of social networks are not a case).

- Development and application of skills and hidden irrational untapped potential by making it more explicit and hoard the boundary between paid work and hobbies.
- Improving the measurement of results achieved according to the ratio revenue / commitment: The parameters for the achievement of personal goals is not just a business tool for follow-up on merit. Of course, it is not easy. But it can become so, if you add a more responsible behavior with appropriate social policies.

Meanwhile, you need a mental preparation. Just think that living on income is not a crime!

Moreover, the conviction of a more relaxed way of life is very old. And has become anachronistic.

It's been more than 200 years, since the holders of capital have begun to fill with insults those who lived on a pension. The workers, however, have always aspired to gain time and to live according to their needs. Living on income is a deep aspiration, ancestral, which should be released. we should feel no more uncomfortable if, by reducing the working time and pursue our own hobbies or our family, the best that we can do in twenty-four hours is read a newspaper or play chess. We must resist the shame of being idle, the legacy of social conditioning lasted for centuries. Yes, someone will be fraught with boredom, laziness and a sense of unease. In that case, it is important to keep in mind a "special" time stolen from work is time well spent, because it useful to meet the wishes of happiness and to devote oneself to passions.

And then you must take into consideration other aspects. Reducing the work reduces taxes, even appreciably. Then, it is easier to make less compromises, impose minimum conditions, request a personalized management of the service times. Taking less in financial terms can, however, lets more easily choose a job that corresponds closely to one's own wishes and attitudes. In this sense, many people carry the same job as before but with less intensity, through the formula of advice or agency. Still others have transformed the previous work in an entirely independent and even fundamental of the former profession tainted by conflicts of interest and commercial compromises. Realize your passion will always give you a deep satisfaction, even if sometimes not enough to your financial sustainability. Hence the importance to impose a way of life and learning to "reevaluate" its intangible assets, know how to "price". Redefine the concepts of wealth and poverty and measures of well-being. Restructure its assets, it would be the better lifestyle choice. Redistribute wealth within their own family, especially between generations, in anticipation of small donations to life what was intended as a legacy to post-mortem. Relocate their lives in a peaceful and less expensive. Reduce unnecessary energy consumption, as well as taxes and three-time work four hours a day. Reuse and recycle, to recover value, ideas, knowledge and relationships that can bring wealth.

Use the time in a playful manner and always in company of others. even in U.S. there is extensive literature on time-management of the idle life. We share most of the planning approach itself, which resembles the classical self-discipline designed to leave no empty one day and rather inclined to make a mark for every day living. It is recommended to write a list of wishes (Anthony Robbins teaches ...), so keep them in mind, well in sight. It is also considered useful to construct a weekly plan of activities and a small memo of what you want and you can do, thereby discouraging from wasting time, because you will be ashamed to admit that everything you did yesterday was the full of gasoline and spend a few hours watching television. Not neglect the little tips, like "do not read the newspaper or send mail early in the morning because they confuse your brain with a bunch of disjointed ideas." The important thing, beyond all the suggestions, is not to play too close with these patterns, the routine learned on the job. And live the transition to new life with peace of mind. Despite the hardships of a financial nature that, suddenly, the change could give.

Think of the panic in the face of some sustainability, because after calculations there are unexpected new arrivals, revenue, more outlets. The advice is always in the direction of rationalization, which may be followed by a conscious revision of certain elements of your model: a lower provision for succession, cost reductions, a reorganization of the portfolio. As you can see the transition to a more comfortable life can only occur through a serious plan. And only making calculations, predictions, we can afford to maintain a more relaxed lifestyle. Never, therefore, head shots to choose to live on income, that is not an invitation to live a life of luxury, but to live in a slow and uncompetitive.

For this reason, the magic word, which is essential to switch to an idle life, is to plan. Choose appropriately also the time when changing modus vivendi. Why, for example, it is preferable not to begin to live on income after a bereavement, an unhappy time. And precisely quantify the resources needed to live when you reduce time and earnings from job.

Time is the most precious thing a man can spend

Theophrastus

OUT OF DEBT

Important in the early stages is to learn how to: get out of debt, to control your consumption, manage your assets in a conscious way, enjoy the financial techniques of inaction, to create social capital within families and communities. More specifically: not to remain alone, even communicate with others, do not use forms of consumer credit, eliminate credit cards, have a conservative approach to wealth-protection, not even become a major creditor, monitor the effects and reward yourself for your results. So, once you understand the need to change a life mediaworld-nalized to achieve independence through sobriety, you should start to consider: whether to seek early retirement or moving into the semi-retirement, how to make a profit from your properties, how to manage a mortgage. And all this, having in mind that in order to life on income you must avoid waste and running emulation, also you should accept the gift. Finally, you can change the very way of life, but it is an exercise that is refined over time. Chekhov and Aristotle say good: "Excellence, such as vulgarity, is not an isolated act, but a behavior." The strategy of downshifting (Voluntary Simplicity), it's a crucial element, but it will not be enough to live on income. The important thing is constant vigilance, because there can always be something out of the budget: a renewal of furniture, the bathroom to be redone, a dentist, a holiday that wants its costs, unforeseen taxes a year, and in Brazil bureaucracy and taxes are sometimes unpredictable in these respects ... we recommend the Practical Guide" Investing in Brazil! What to do and what not to do .... " We must avoid basing a income life plan live only on the idea of reducing consumptions. It takes more. You need: choices about what you want to leave to others in life and after, fair and honest estimates of the availability of family property, an effective approach to pension plans, a constant control of its assets, by making it revenue, then a commitment protection of public property and the proper use of common property. Often, the area in which we move with greater spontaneity, is the most insidious. It protects and reassure us, but only in appearance. The objectives of the job, the synthesis of many experiences and professional life, is, in fact, inspire out of this area of false comfort, to know that other people have made it and explain how they did it. For this reason we reported in the book true stories of some of these people.
There is who can do this step alone. However, there are those who need a confrontation with a friend or a professional. Who, again, is more difficult and needs a psychotherapist, because it requires a change at the same time broader and deeper, having more unconscious resistance. It is not important, however, the way you get to change. Fundamental is make

it, to leave behind, if you really want, that gray zone of stasis, impotence to act, and be something different.

"This is the only life we have: we might as well gamble at best, no regrets later and arrive at a true harmony between intentions and deeds." Many times the change comes from external inputs. And it is automatic. The economy and society change together, the existence of individuals, relationships, hierarchies of values. And in this global crisis, no one can afford to remain a mere observer of the phenomenon. He is forced to be protagonists. Indeed, it is better to be agents of change rather than passively suffer it. This seems to be the real key to build a life that resembles as much as possible. Think of how changed the labor market. Many thirty-aged people do not know what it means to have a 'fixed place', the primary aspiration of previous generations, with the "eternal" activity they could start a family. Build a house. Today, the permanent position leaves more room for private initiatives. So we should grab the bull by the horns, take back control of our destiny to address it as best suited to each. Of course, all this has a price. The changes bring pain with them, because they mess up the lives of those who face them. So what? The important thing is that they are weighted, measured, gradual. And most importantly, "recognized". In this sense, we must learn to listen, which is not easy at all but essential. So the push for change should never be underestimated. Can arise from negative emotions (anxiety, frustration, feelings of inadequacy), but they should be investigated, because have a deeper meaning. The life we lead is not often suitable for us. The "crisis" may well become a great opportunity for renewal, a healthy 'cold shower' in which to find motivation, strength and creativity. And this without giving weight to age. Often, the 'salvation', which is perceived at an older age may reside in these six words:

"Leaving is often much better than staying."

YOU HAVE DECIDED TO ESCAPE FROM YOUR COUNTRY?

For many jobs the physical presence "in office" is becoming more marginal, while the Internet and the computer can give a "daily" presence in a company. The tourist starts to become a resident. The choice of a new dimension prevails over the surface of curiosity. In short, we change home, country, place of life, habits forever or for a few months a year. Spending a lot less money than at home and living better a lot. Of course, a flexible escape, affordable for all budgets. Providing of course to cut some arm of the bridge and bravery necessary.

How many psychologists say a happy change is not the destruction of the former life, but an evolution that saves and improves the best. In fact, we do not like the expression and / or common places as: give up everything, run away, change of life and never come back, etc ... The secret, if there is a secret, is to plan and to ask, as you are doing right now reading this book. Preparation for the choice of a happy "flight" requires certain conditions. First, the knowledge of the place, where to go. Brazil is a continent, not forget. Then you have to think about their budget, taste its climate, the ability to adapt to local cuisine, even your health. And speaking of health dispel some commonplaces. And that is that in Latin America health care is like third world. Doctors with proved experience and ability are working in the network of hospitals and medical clinics, since of course you have to pay private services from time to time or join a health insurance policy.

The British, the French, the Americans have their DNA in the habit of mobility to the colonies, even by middle – high classes. Many former exotic lands of these nations are still very popular within our European friends, so that - let's face it - they never stopped to consider some overseas territories as their land.

The philosophy that drives the "flight" is simple " Between looking for an insecure job at home and looking for a temporary work abroad, I choose the latter and at least I'm enjoying the tropical sun."

So it's easy to predict not only an increase of the phenomenon, but also its "young-ilization", as the difficulties of economic homeland increases. There is a positive aspect in this phenomenon, given the new awareness that life should be lived with fullness and creativity. And both young people and sixty-aged people think so. But there is also some downside. Many of the Northeast coast of Brazil and not only are experiencing a cementing and over-building fate equal to that recorded in the 60's and 70's on our coasts.

Tasteless and unscrupulous contractors compete offering low-cost apartments and cottages to the European market, regardless of the environmental damage they produce. The meaning of "escape" should be investigated in the choice to weave a relationship with the population of the new place that you choose and, above all, try to be helpful with many possible forms of aid and solidarity.

SOCIETY IS CHANGING

Anger: you may define it the evil of the century and you do not exaggerate. Look around. It seems that aggression connotes every daily gesture. Stalking, harassment, bullying, yelling on television guests, tenants who make a table conflict, reality shows made for the purpose of angering the participants. It has become difficult even to endure the noise of neighbors. So much that you maybe take the gun and shoot at them. And the media? Amplify some disturbing details to attract the attention of readers. But what is happening and, especially, will it get worse? Maybe it will, if we can not re-size the daily problems and revise the scale of our values and if we continue to live in isolation.

It's a primary emotion (anger) as joy and pain, which is part of the founding of the human emotions, and it catches us, more or less constantly throughout the course of life. It can also be an alarm that warns of a threat from outside, but also of something that is on the rise within us at the moment, in our brains. It is not an emotion that has a negative connotation. It may in fact be a strong stimulus to achieve a goal. It may be the impetus to act and react to unpleasant circumstances for us. Other times can be an unbearable feeling to have suffered an injustice and in this case it gives us the charge to try to gain the respect from others and ourselves.

If we use it to achieve a goal, strengthen a decision, to fight injustice, no harm. If instead it is just a way of reacting to frustration, causing repeated mental wounds, in others and in ourselves, will obviously be harmful. Have a look at young people and at new violence that affects them. In the society of the past was unthinkable that a fourteen years young man was leaving in the evening around the city with a knife in his pocket, going to use alcohol and drugs. There were no rave parties, there were clubs that were opening at midnight. Fourteen children were in school. About the school: there were rules, meritocracy, punishments, rules, and behold, all things gone away, so that bullying and transgression flourish. There was no Internet, and then the boys could not put their "good" movies on the net, could not make themselves visible as negative heroes.

Television programs were beautiful, uplifting, there were no papers and "throner", no unattainable models intended for young people. First there was not the opportunity to aspire to so many status symbols, to rob a companion for the mobile phone fashion.

The traffic was lower and thus the "rage" from traffic was smaller. Women do not abandon their husbands (there was no divorce) and then there was not the murderous rage of some men frustrated that more and more use the stalking in a killing spree.

And so on. Yes, it is this society that creates this new rage. The women once held in all their anger with the effect of suffering from different diseases (colitis, dermatitis, etc..) And feel constantly frustrated and depressed. Today they manage to be aggressive, but it is a choice, because its biology does not have it, it lacks the large amount of human testosterone, the hormone that leads to aggression. The selection takes place unfortunately when the woman has to make his way in the world of job, when she gets power. This female aggression is a sin, does not suit, frightens. It would be better to find other outlets to vent their anger.

The purpose of work is to gain free time.

Aristotle

CHANGE LIFE IS AT OUR DOOR

A brief history: Luke is an important executive of a multinational corporation: it has a fabulous salary and all the privileges of the world, but is tired of his job to devote 14 hours a day, to spend half his time traveling, he is tired of useless meetings and frustrated projects.

Every time I see him he tells me some new plan of life, new ideas that go through his head that would allow him to be able to change his life. Some ideas are truly impossible, but most have a meaning and, if only he seriously proposes them, he would be able to do so. Instead, as soon as he lists them he always finds some excuse, something that prevent the realization of his projects. Children, mortgage, costs ... there is always something that prevents him from seriously believing in the possibility to change his life. Maybe that's why every speech about it begins with "Ah, if I win the lottery..."

"We are responsible for our lives. Our behavior is a result of our decisions, not our conditions" (Stephen Covey)

Sooner or later we all wanted to see how our life would change if we win the lottery. But you do not win the lottery almost never, and making our plans depend on this possibility means to be mistaken. Enter into a betting shop and observe a "crowd of people" who nervously "scratch and sctatch again", heads down and bowed rectangular cards it's one of the sad shows you can watch in recent years. Changing life does not depend on chance, but on our will. It depends, above all, on how seriously we want it and how, after we resigned ourselves of this, we can make a good project, addressing this process with the rigor and method in order to make it become a reality and not remain a mere fantasy.

Changing life supposes we are able to look within ourselves and able to analyze all the aspects that generate dissatisfaction. Supposed we are able to rearrange all the pieces to rebuild a project that we feel responsible, and whom we want face.

We all have a dream that we would like to see realized because we would be very happy and it would give a new meaning to our lives. Identification is crucial to begin the process of change, and it is sometimes difficult, because we are slaves of fear, doubt and responsibility that cloud our view and prevent us from seeing this dream. Often what we want is not unreachable, it can even take the form of activities that we perform only sporadically, or complementary to our profession, but we never would think of that as an option for a possible change of life.

Other times we search our past for what once made us happy and satisfied.

In any case, all the dreams that we can identify will help us. This is because dreams must be achievable in order to change our life, and that means they must meet at least three criteria:
- at first it must be an activity that we do well (it's much easier to be realized in something we already know rather than deal with trying to get some experience in something we do not know)
- secondly, it must be something that make us earn money (to avoid earning-less romantic ideas), yes, the kiosk on the beach and exporting "piadina romagnola" do not give a true economic support...)
- thirdly, it must be something that makes us feel happy and fulfilled (to do something we like is the best guarantee of success).
To achieve our dreams we must be able to reorganize our time. Often we convince ourselves we don't have enough time to do all the things we like, but in reality what happens is a bad use of our time. We must learn to prioritize everything that makes our dreams come true. Priority is to move the key to control your time.
We must stop wasting time on useless things and commitments without effect, and this is only beginning to learn to say no to anything that does not help to make our project possible. Of course it's never easy to say no, because nobody likes to be disliked or disappoint others. For this, however we pay a high price, that we can not deal with what really interests us, and we do not realize that we give up our plans for tasks or commitments that do not interest us.
We must first decide what we need to reach our new goal, and forget everything we can do without. We are used to surround and search a lot more of what we really need: we often seek in the objects we buy a form of compensation to our unhappiness and dissatisfaction coming from work, stress and tension. Other times the external pressure convinces us to believe that those are the things we absolutely need. No doubt there is nothing so beautiful and wonderful as anything that you does not possess, but as soon as we buy it the illusion vanishes, we have never thought of that? Furthermore, everything that builds up in our lives brings new work with it: what we buy has to be maintained, cared for, sheltered, protected ... so over to buy unnecessary items, which once seemed necessary, we become slaves.
We need to understand what we really need to implement our plan: it is better to take a trip that can help us not to get in trouble for having badly chosen what to bring with us. In this way we will avoid concerns and simplify our lives and we will be able to find happiness where it really should be searched for. The more we are obsessed with our work, the more we focus only on ourselves, ignoring our relationship and moving away from people. It is ironic to see how we can spend our time and our efforts in job relations at the

expense of those which represent the most important, the fundamentals. We must learn to take care of our relationships, to dedicate time and effort, because these relationships are the only ones that will allow us to grow and develop as people. The construction and care of relations is a long-term investment.

We need to understand who are the people more connected with us, who are those people that we would like as fellow travelers in our new life. Those people will be the ones who will make us feel good and feel good to know, the ones that will help us and that we will know how to help. It is obviously a work of selecting and opening ourselves to too many people is the best guarantee of failure, and the effort required to maintain friendly relations with many people risks to choke us.

Knowing how to build and to be able to take care of an interpersonal relationship means being able to give up grudges, let go of resentments and friction, and this is necessary in order to create the space we need to maintain relationships that we take care of. This is mainly because bearing someone a grudge lets him have great power to us.

Being able to see the positive side of people and forget the flaws is a good step forward, we have both, and being able to recognize them within other people will also help us in our relationship with ourselves.

"When you win your fear you conquer your life" (Robin S. Sharma) Fear is the great brake on any proposed change of life. It knows how to surprise us at the worst moment and in the worst way, exposing in an essential way the dangers we are exposed to and undermining all of our decisions.

Fear makes us lose a lot of opportunities: because of the fear we lock up in our circle of security and give up to explore new ways and new possibilities. We lose our vitality and our ability to judge.

We must be able to look fear in the eyes and not allow it to condition our life. But we can not (and should not) remove the fear from our lives, why is fear that keeps us on guard, but we must be able to identify its signs and be able to know how to stop in time when it goes too far. We must let it protect us, but without allowing it humbling ourselves.

If we control our fear we will be able to explore new horizons, to try to do what we wanted for some time, but we never dared to face, we began so to let out our true human potential.

Check the fear will make change possible

Anonymous

TIPS FOR LIFE CHANGE

The phenomenon of downshifting, included in the broader concept of simple living, living in simplicity.

A practice not just recently. In the seventies, philosophers such as Jean Baudrillard (The consumer society, 1970) and André Gorz (Environment & Policy, 1975) theorized the need of décroissance, decrease, based on the awareness of individually and globally unsustainability of too fast development rates.

Today, as thirty years ago, partisans of the slowness think we should do the best possible and not so quickly as possible.

But who are the supporters of going slow? Professionals with a good job above all, good graduation, various specializations. They can choose. They have this privilege. They do this by opting for a lifestyle on a human scale, as "green".

These are people who decided to give up marathons of stressful jobs to have more free time to devote to family, to their hobbies, friends. Men and women who face a global economic crisis, the depletion of the planet's wealth and drying of their lives, they begin to reset their own lifestyle. To give an impression more "Eastern", leaner, less determined by impulse, sometimes by manic consumption. And less "connected".

The downshifter is the one who recovers his emotional, depriving them of chances for career success and money. And the one who invests on the concept of happiness, waiting for individual choices become fashionable, able to transform our society and our rigid division of job. Well, we find a real example by the phenomenon that, by mistake, many sociologists suggest the term "mother-men". In fact they are the fathers who are catching their emotional dimension, denied for too long. What do they do? Shorten their working hours to spend more time with their children instead of their companions.

How to take it slow?

Of course, to review the basics of life, an ambitious goal. It's not easy to stop "inflation" of working days, giving more space to the affective sphere and take a more 'environmentally friendly' dimension. But you can try. And the password must start to be for everyone "to work less, spend less, consume less, to have more time for themselves". To be idle. And maybe to be more creative. You should turn into craftsmen who work slowly, but with care and passion.

Stop to unnecessary shopping, which often becomes a second job, a run that deceives us, because it makes us feel alive, as productive. Stop to all illusions. Few things to better savor the pleasure. No coincidence that one of the interests of downshifters is diet. Down with fast food and frozen food. Better to eat dishes prepared with one's own hands and more genuine. So you will be rewarding and save more.

If saving money, living better and in a healthier way, respecting themselves and environment looks complicated, we could look at the Chinese women that still have healthy habits. Yes, the fair sex of that economic power that goes fast, but not in a hurry, can be a good model. There, women do not throw the water used to boil rice. They reuse it, because it's rich in starch, to water the plants. Residues of soap they use for bathing are combined and processed in floor cleaners. And then, to wet rooms in China, the women put the soaked bread on radiators. A little bit as it was here twenty years ago.

The slow economy, capitalism with a conscience, which the Western powers should look at, perhaps, more closely. This is not to go back but, for example, to review our wealth indicators by region. When Western governments will use the "GDHap", the rate of Gross Domestic Happiness, to measure the growth of a country? Bhutan has introduced it long time ago.

Bhutan * (full name: Kingdom of Bhutan) is a small mountainous state in Asia (47,000 km ^{2}, estimated about 650,000 inhabitants in 2005, the capital Thimphu) located in the Himalayas. It is bordered to the north by China and south India. Bhutan is the only country that professes the official religion as a form of Buddhism called Mahayana. Buddhism has played a key role in the history and development of social structures, still plays an important role both for the general weight of the clergy in society (until a few decades ago, they had monopoly of culture, as only in monasteries you could receive education), for the importance given to religious values also in political action.
* Source Wikipedia

Then try to exit the fast-forward, catch my breath. Let's reset our lives in another register. And Brazilians are the masters of all the art of living slow. Stop then to thick agendas up in agony. Stop to uncontrollable frenzy of career and stress by overwork. Stop to writings on the fly as sms saving on vowels and punctuation. And stop as well to the races to last technological gadget, or the umpteenth pair of shoes, as long in Brazil you wear Havajanas 24h, 365 days a year. Then go home and discover that shopping does not bring happiness.

Here is an article that appeared in the Spanish site www.univision.com signed Maria Jesus Rivas. Can we change our lives? After we have relegated our dreams to last place of an unsatisfactory life and made of routine, you can still try to live well, satisfied and happy? Apparently yes, by following a few simple techniques.

THE TIME TO SAY ENOUGH IS ENOUGH

Isabel, a 43 years old endocrinologist left his hospital to become a nun, high school teacher Kim decided to underwent the operation that would make him a woman, at 47 years old Miguel chose to abandon his career as a chef in a famous restaurant and dedicate himself to the renovation of small Spanish villages, Clara was a judge and today is a classical ballet teacher and a dancer. Their time to say "Enough" arrived, and they decide to start a new life from scratch. It was not enough to readjust a little bit in everyday life, make it more acceptable, they needed a radical change, well thought, well priced, which would have totally changed their way of life. But they were looking for happiness, and doing so they found it. Some change their sex, country, culture, religion, change their profession or other activity, but one thing is common to all: wonder, disbelief and surprise of those people close to them. Change is a difficult decision to make - say experts - but once you have decided you surprise yourself at first, you who chose to change. A total change of life, leaving everything behind? Sooner or later we all think of it when we are oppressed by routine and stress. The real case of Isabel, Miguel, Clara, Kim, however, show us you can delete everything, change radically, to create a new life. But first it is necessary and essential to know very well. Although most of the time you does not need a radical change to improve life everyday, but it is enough to introduce small attentions, scientists have recently discovered that the desire to leave everything and start from scratch coincides with the so-called "crisis of middle-age", that occurs when you take stock of how you lived and what you made. The radical change is a difficult step to be taken at any age and often the emotional ties serve as a screen. Inertia, family obligations, the illusion of security, and insecurity of a job are obstacles along the path to change, not to mention the fear and anxiety that such a radical decision implies. Despite everything, however - experts say - you can choose to change your fate, leaving behind dissatisfaction and malaise, after you have carefully and deeply thought, and following the appropriate procedure. More and more people feel themselves victims of an inactive lifestyle, boring and feeling they have lost control of their lives, their own destiny. When this malaise is strong people feel trapped in a reality that does not have choices, they want to move on, trying to create a life that more reflects their dreams and desires.

First we must analyze, identify and bring to the root causes and attitudes that are maintained in case of success or failure, because you have to make major changes within these insecurities, fears or accommodating behaviors. Change the shape without changing the substance leads only and always towards the same conclusions. If you aim to a change that makes your life rewarding you can fall into the very common error to idealize your own future, imagining a fantastic paradise and losing sight of reality. The more the project is far from our real possibility, the more the disappointment will be close. Living in the country, changing job, moving to Brazil are possible changes only if you are able to recognize themselves in your projects, otherwise you risk to fall into the trap of a false change. Often those who are bored with their life create the idea of vanish, to leave everything and start all over again, like the people who decide to leave the job in the city and move to a small country. It is an escape, and when you run away from a conflict, this will come again; it is better to recognize it, address it and then decide whether you still want to radically change your life.

Another common mistake is to try to change everything so that nothing changes. It 's the case of those who change jobs due to expectations: being in a more pleasant place, having more free time to dedicate to something more persuasive. In fact, the malaise that generates these thoughts does not begin in the work field, but in themselves and then is translated into a series of habits that come in addition to daily routine. The first step to do is an inner journey, discovery, re-find one's identity, its inner nature. According to psychologists, "if after you have thoroughly analyzed this decision you still believe that the distance between desire and the real possibility of its realization is huge, then you are ready to face change and all its consequences. A successful change is not a destruction, but an evolution that saves and improves the best." So you should always design a precise destination, make a plan to achieve it, be realistic, creative and flexible, without improvising. We must not settle for self-deception and move our illness from a geographical point to another.

To give us a second chance (changing jobs, going around the world, going to university or engaging in humanitarian work) we suggest six basis points that can help us making life more satisfying. First of all you must be able to distinguish between existential malaise and a momentary anxiety . If the difference between our aspirations and the reality is considerable, will be better worth to analyze our life and re-plan what makes us unhappy. Sometimes misery is given by being fairly objective or not seeing clearly what we would do or be, then we need to think, to break the inertia and put changes into effect with the right decision. Often this simple reflection avoids disappointment. If however the decision to radically change life resist, you must plan well. We must let us know each other well and understand what you really want, and weigh well the desire for change. Anxiety can be a stimulus, but may also block the ability to think rationally. You should thoroughly analyze the resources (economic but also of adaptability, and creativity) to make sure we can face any difficulties well. The project is then planned: it must be realistic, sensible and according to your means. You have to face your limits not to fall in the mistakes already made. You must obtain the necessary information in order to help the project, to avoid that it becomes a fantasy. Speaking as much as possible with friends and family helps a lot: expose the expectations, the results to be obtained, the projects. This constant talk about it will cause the project to acquire even more power and change reality and allows you to detect any errors, comments or opportunities not yet addressed. The fact that many people try to dissuade those who want to leave it all creates the need for a solid project and relevant argument. Changing our lives is not a choice without danger. Let you the chance to return. Calculating the risks and accepting the possibility of making mistakes should be a prerequisite for learning from one's mistakes, improving the alternative projects of the future. Then we go from theory to practice: armed with patience and perseverance, without being guided too much by impulse and improvisation, and carefully considering what has been learned till today, always knowing how adapt oneself well and getting over the crisis and changes in one's projects, we will be ready to face a radical change with all that it entails.

HOW TO SAVE YOUR EURO MONEY AND EARN IN BRAZIL

First, investing in Brazil means automatically earning more than the average investment in old Europe.

Perhaps investing in India or China could make more money, but because you may need to travel to these countries sooner or later, in the case of industrial or real estate investments, we prefer Brazil to China or India. An interesting comment of Bloomberg News on the rise of SELIC, of 0.75 percentage points, from 8.75 to 9.5%, showing that Brazil is the first South American nations, as well as the third among the 20 Richer nations, which increases the interest rate after the financial crisis, the article points out that this increase will be the first of four or maybe five or six that the Central Bank will decide in the coming months.

The estimated total is +4 percentage points between this year and next, or a total 12.75%.

This is to bring inflation within the parameters, or around 4.5%. For those who want to earn in Brazil is confirmed what has been said in previous chapters on how to create a financial income. If you still have some savings in euro you shall not lose any more time. Transfer everything in R $ and invest in real estate and funds related to DI index.

The real will be enhanced even against the euro, and the euro is a target of fierce speculation because of crisis in EU countries. Thus there are no positive signs for the euro: only strong negative signals. Attention to what is happening in Greece and the rest of Europe, do not believe in easy solutions to the problem.

The Central Bank of Brazil became the first in Latin America to increase borrowing costs in more than a year, bringing its interest rate higher than the forecasts of most analysts, without reporting the rate of future increases. In a unanimous vote, the board of the bank increased the Selic rate to 9.5 percent from a record 8.75 percent. Policy makers, in a press release of a single sentence that accompanies their decision, said that the increase gives continuity to the process of adjustment of monetary conditions for the economic outlook in order to ensure convergence of inflation to the target trajectory .

The prospects of interest rate "depend on how inflation expectations behave," told Pedro Paulo Silveira, chief economist at "Gradual corretor" in a telephone interview from Sao Paulo. "The central bank will raise rates for at least four meetings, but it could be five or six."

The bank acted with forecasts that let Latin America's largest economy expand at the fastest pace this year than in the entire last two decades, prompting increases in consumer prices as far as the government's target of 4.5 percent.

EARN A FINANCIAL INCOME IN BRAZIL

In the previous chapter we showed how, by investing approximately
€ 250,000 you can buy a villa, a compact car and invest the rest in bank stocks in order to build an income of R $ 3,000 per month (about 1310 euro) enough to live in a town in northeast Brazil.
In this chapter we intend to answer the many questions we have received and which examine primarily the latter aspect, the investment bank. Many people ask us what this investment is exactly, if they are safe and whether there are particular requirements to do so.
We begin by recalling that since the investment is in local currency, it can be done only if you have a bank account in Brazil. This is easily done if you have the permanent visa, while is difficult, but not impossible, if you do not have such a visa.
In Brazil, all the banks offer credit certificates (CDB) or funds linked to the cost of money (SELICE) today to 8.75%. Typically, the gross yield is around 95% of this index over the taxation of 15%. Finally, a 7.5% net. Until a few years ago SELICE was over 20% then gradually reduced until the current value. By the end of May 2010 is expected to lift interest rates that should remain at 25.11% by end of 2010 or a 10% equity.
Financial products associated with that index are basically three: CDB, savings (Caderneta de Poupanca) and Investment Funds. The CDB are real credit certificates issued by the bank, they may have an interest in pre and post set. If the investor believes that interest rates will fall in the future (this is the case now) it makes sense to invest in CDB set as the fixed rate will not suffer because of the reduction. If, by contrast, a rise is expected, is worth investing to post-fixed, that will have a floating rate and will benefit from the increase of the same. I mean the opposite of a mortgage. The guarantee of a CBD depends on the credibility and soundness of the Bank in addition to being guaranteed by the Credit Guarantee Fund (FGC) to the amount of R $ 60,000 for Tax Code / CPF.

The taxation on the performance of the CDB shall follow the following table:
- 22.5% within 180 days
- 20% from 181 to 360 days
- 17.5% from 361 to 720 days
- 15% over 720 days
In order to prevent speculation in the short term there is a further decreasing tax (IOF) for those who wish to withdraw the investment within the first 30 days.
Starting 31 days such taxation is zero and remain the only published rates in the table above. There are no management fees to be paid. Credible and solid banks in Brazil are the BANCO DO BRASIL, BRADESCO, Itau / Unibanco, ABN AMRO REAL (Santander Group), etc ...

The savings account, or Poupanca, shall be remunerated according to an index TR (reference rate) plus a monthly rate published by the Bank. It's exempt from taxation. It 's the solution preferred by small investors because of its simplicity. It has the same warranty as the CDB and its efficiency is on average lower than the CBD.

The investment funds are financial instruments that allow you to invest in a basket of stocks and bonds in different proportions managed by experienced analysts from the Bank itself. The funds which we refer in particular are those attached to the so-called index which is precisely tied to Selice. The taxation of funds is more detailed than that of the CDB. In particular, funds are divided into:
Short-term funds taxed at 22.5% within 180 days and 20% over 180 days.
Long-term funds taxed as the CDB
Equity funds taxed at 15%
The funds are generally treated as long-term funds. Unlike the CBD which are taxed only at the time of redemption, the Funds in the short and long term are taxed every six months and at the time of redemption. The equity funds are taxed only on the contrary at the time of redemption that continue to apply regardless of the time and also do not pay the ransom when IOF carried out within the first 30 days.
Unlike the CBD, also funds have management fees varying with the type of investment. The committees, for example, can go from 0.8% to 5.5% in the case of Banco do Brasil depending largely on the amount invested. The more you invest, the more commission will be reduced. Finally, the funds do not get any sort of guarantee from the Bank, nor even of the Credit Guarantee Fund.

This book is dedicated to all those who dream of moving to Brazil and do not know where to begin nor if it is feasible.

Suppose for the moment that you have already solved the problem of visas otherwise your staying on Brazil territory will be reduced to a maximum of six months per year. Have permanent visa will facilitate the task of obtaining the opening of a Brazilian bank account, otherwise this can be difficult if not impossible.

Having said that to live on income in Brazil as in any other place you need to control costs regardless of the monthly amount available. If you can discipline it will take you only 30 euro per day, if you cannot 300 euros will not be enough.

Therefore, this guide will divide into two parts, first we will analyze how to live on income or how rationally spend a certain amount per month generated by an investment in real estate and second to generate a financial income in Brazil.

People living on income generally known his revenue with great precision, and therefore just needs discipline and a simple tool to balance revenue with expenditure.

This tool is a simple spreadsheet like Excel. Divide the sheet in fourteen columns. The first will contain items of expenditure, the following 12 values of the costs broken down by last month the annual totals. The same can obviously be done with pencil and paper but you will lose the advantages of simplicity and the possibility of correction formulas (for example to calculate the total at year end).

An example of items of expenditure: mortgage, condo, gas, water, electricity, fixed telephone, mobile phone, internet, taxes, fuel, maintenance, clothing, furniture, gifts, entertainment (books, DVDs, motel ...), hygiene staff, cleaning house, food, restaurants, travel, health, social etc ...

The hard part, but necessary, is in the record on their daily agenda expenditure and return later this month on the spreadsheet. In a few months we will be without an idea of our average monthly expenditure. At this point, extrapolating over the year, we forecast our financial needs. Basically what revenue we need to balance the outputs. If the rent is already known it will be shaping the future costs in order to bring them into the budget.

In the case of Brazil, admitted to being a couple already owning a small apartment you will need approximately R $ 3,000 for living, or about 1,310 euros.

To obtain an income of R $ 3,000 per month, R $ 36,000 a year, investing in a secure financial application, we need at least $ 450,000 invested at 8% net.

So with the money earned, for example, from the sale of an apartment in Italy, about 250,000 Euros, about R $ 575,000, we can: move to Brazil, buying a furnished apartment to R $ 150,000 and invest R $ 425,000 in Treasury bills or equivalent.

Of course these are averages. For some R $ 3,000 may be few and therefore must balance its investment by placing, for example, 15% on an equity fund. This figure could even reach 30% if the time is propitious.

EARN POINTS ON THE BRAZILIAN REAL

Brazil's economy is emerging between those with a higher growth prospects. The British consultancy agency EIU (Economist Intelligence Unit), in its ranking of the best economies in the world, put "carioca" country at eighth place ahead Spain, Canada, India and Russia. The strength of growth in the economy of Rio is also found in the effervescence of the Exchange Securities. The stock market has almost come close to the peaks reached in 2008 before the outbreak of the global financial crisis and the same currency, the real, is the highest of the last eight years against the dollar and especially against the euro.

Looking at these circumstances, and at the growth prospects of the Brazilian economy, the bet on further appreciation of the carioca against the European currency for the coming months can win. The problem is that it can be a little complicated for a small investor to be able to invest in Brazilian real. Deutsche Bank offers a solution to the Express by Rivers (ID code Isin: DE000DB7LPB1), a certificate that allows you to focus on strengthening Brazilian currency against the euro.

This new certificate was issued in late May 2010, focuses on the exchange rate of euro-Brazilian real, that those who buy it earns with an appreciation of the currency against the euro carioca. The certificate, which expires April 30, 2012, offers a coupon of 5% for each six-month period from date of issue, provided that in the real dates of November 1 2010, May 1 2011 and April 30 2012 has not dropped against the euro under a certain price level (strike), which will be determined the next April 29 2010.

It's guaranteed the repayment of principal at maturity, provided that it the barrier set at 155% of the strike remains untouched, till the final valuation date. If the real on that date will be devalued more than 55% compared with the values determined on April 29, the capital return will not be 100 euro nominal, required to purchase a certificate, but the investment will become comparable to the direct purchase of the Brazilian currency .

CITIES OF BRAZIL

Whether this is your first visit or your hundredth visit to Brazil, the fact is that Brazil has so much to see and do for tourists that there is no better time or better place than other! So, to try to help you plan your holiday in Brazil, below the top destinations in Brazil (no particular order of preference):

NATIONAL PARK OF THE AMAZON

Stretching for 7 states out of total 27 Brazilian states, "The Green Hell", covers nearly 40 percent of the territory of Brazil. Although the Amazon rainforest extending into neighboring countries (particularly in Bolivia, Colombia, Guyana and Peru), it is in Brazil that most of the tourists is concentrated to marvel at this natural wonder. Among the activities to do in the Amazon there are bird watching, trekking / hiking, climbing, rafting etc ... Without a doubt, a tour to Brazil is incomplete without a visit to the Amazon.

THE FALLS IGUASSU

They are described as one of the seven natural wonders of the world. On the Parana River, the falls act as a natural border between the countries of Brazil, Argentina and Paraguay and compose a total of 275 waterfalls. The best time to see the waterfalls of "Iguacu" is between October and December and you are strongly advised to stay at least one night here before moving on to your next destination!

RIO DE JANEIRO

The word "exotic" captures the essence of Rio, the second most populous city in Brazil (after Sao Paulo)! But Rio is also chaotic, sophisticated, open, friendly, lively and relaxed. There are all these features literally "rolled" into one! Most people in Rio combines sun, sea and surf. Although Rio is all this, it is also much more.

If you are looking for a combination of beaches, sports, sun, exotic parks and gardens, with spectacular views of the mountains, a little dance and cocktails, Rio is for you. Rio de Janeiro has a majestic beauty, including a beautiful bay with dazzling beaches and mountains covered with tropical vegetation. With the establishment of Brasilia in 1960, Rio has ceased to be the capital of Brazil, but is still a major cultural capital with many museums with a wide range of art and information about life and the Brazilian culture. The city is one of the most densely populated on earth, with 6 million inhabitants. Rio loves the sun and its famous beaches are free to all, with surfing as a popular pastime. The legendary Copacabana beach is lively, full of people intent on playing beach volleyball with the samba in the background. The promenade is filled with stands where you can drink any type of tropical smoothie with the ubiquitous coconut water and street vendors offering all the necessary items to take advantage of the beach.

Another beach, Ipanema, is known to be young and hip, with numerous boutiques and is the premier of the wealthy classes in Rio. On the cultural side, the Museum of National History in Rio as many other museums and cultural centers financed by private individuals are filled with masterpieces and wonderful history. Only the National History Museum has a collection of 30,000 items, including ivory jewelry once owned by the imperial family. At the Monastery of São Bento, you can admire magnificent chandeliers in silver and ceiling paintings dedicated to the Virgin. The Franciscan monastery is lined with gilded wood, with painted ceilings depicting the glorification of St. Francis.

It would take a whole day to watch all the great churches. One of the most important is the baroque cathedral of "Igreja de Nossa Senhora da Gloria" overlooking the city, known for its large dome.

One of the most exciting sites is Corcovado, a mountain with a sheer granite wall topped by "Cristo Redentor" (Christ the Redeemer) statue of over 100 meters that embraces and protects the entire Rio. You can reach the top rack on a train, enjoying a unique view of the beach.

The second and most famous peak is the 'Sugar Loaf', which is equally impressive and gives a different perspective of the city. The "Sugar Loaf", consists of a granite slab at the entrance of Guanabara Bay. From the summit of 1,295 meters, you can see the whole city together with the beaches and the Atlantic Ocean. To climb to the top use a cable that has a length of 4,265 meters. The sunsets are fabulous view from the top.

The festive life of the city reached its peak during the annual Carnival, which benefits the entire city for three days. Music, parties, dances, street parades, dancers in bright costumes and sophisticated.

It 's always time to samba and Carnival in Rio! Carnival is the best time to visit the city, to keep in mind that the city is even more crowded though. The Carnival takes place in February or March, depending on the date of Easter each year. It 'best to get a little' early to enjoy all the attractions. And, above all, to book the hotel at least one year in advance.

Pay special attention to the beaches and night. Leave your passport, jewelry, and most of the cash at your hotel.

PANTANAL

Considered one of the largest nature reserves in the world, every visit to the Pantanal should be carefully planned as the area is not ideal for tourists - in fact there are few existing infrastructure. However, do not let that prevent you to visit the Pantanal because it's really a beautiful place. The fishermen are especially attracted to the Pantanal as it is one of the best places for fishing in South America. But also bird-watching attracts the visitors.

SALVADOR

Salvador, which was once the colonial capital of Brazil, is located in the "Bay of All Saints." Visitors to this wonderful city can enjoy walking the narrow cobblestone streets that have remained the same as when the city was the hub of the slaves in Brazil coming from Africa.

Do not miss a visit to El Salvador "Igreja de Sao Francisco." The interior is lined with gold leaf. Not far from the church is the Farol de Barra, a 16th century fortified lighthouse overlooking the second largest bay in Brazil. The city of Salvador, capital of colonial Brazil for almost two centuries, is today a city of 2 million people. The black African culture, originated by former slaves, is reflected strongly in the culture of the city. In fact, 70 percent of the city's population is Afro-Brazilian. The city was built on two distinct levels, with the residential area in the hills and business area in plains, today is still divided between the top and bottom, with an elevator to take you from one to another. The beaches of El Salvador have been a source of inspiration for writers and musicians. They provide chairs and umbrellas and kiosks selling a range of tempting food and drinks. Many beaches are illuminated at night and the bars and restaurants are famous for their wild nights. Perhaps you'll want to do some shopping at Gran Mercado Modelo as well as visit the many museums. Or, you can venture out to the Fort of Santo Antonio located on the tip of the peninsula, and a ride to the lighthouse and nautical museum, and why not also enjoy the nearby beach.

The choice "hoteliera" in Salvador is very broad, ranging from elegant and luxurious high-rise apartments to family.

The best time to visit the city is between November and April and July (when schools are closed).

It's best not to go around at night in non-core areas, especially if you are alone and, of course, leave jewelry, watches and much of the money in the hotel.

SAO PAULO

There is a word that sums up Sao Paulo "GREAT"! The city is not only the most populous in Brazil, but also the commercial center of Brazil, with some of the biggest skyscrapers in the country. However, visitors to Sao Paulo should not think that is just all work and no play, because once the sun goes down in Sao Paulo the nightlife lights up with some of the most fashionable pubs and clubs all over Brazil, and some argue that in Sao Paulo clubs are more in tune with modern Western styles than Rio!

Sao Paulo is one of the most beautiful jewels of Brazil. This gem is a shining city, which coexists with the culture and industry. Sao Paulo (Sao Paulo) is an amalgam of various cultures that shape the modern face of this Brazilian metropolis.

The city of St. Paul, despite being so popular today, has been for hundreds of years, a small colonial city, and relics of the old city that can still be found all over Sao Paulo.

Today, with 32 shopping malls, hundreds of stores and dozens of roads to four lanes constantly busy, the city is also proud to be the home of two of the 15 most famous zoo in the world, as well as a large number of parks and a botanic garden.

Sao Paulo brings together the best of both worlds, with virtually everything you could want to find in a big city, as well as some things that you would expect. A remarkable fact is the high concentration of immigrants, giving this cosmopolitan metropolis many different faces. Over 1 million Japanese living here gave this city the distinction of being the largest Japanese city outside Japan. Liberdade is the name of the neighborhood where is this center of Japanese culture, is a center of the Asian community, enhanced by picturesque gardens and exotic shops. Do not forget also that 40% of the "Paulistani" is of Italian origin.

To enhance the cultural richness of Sao Paulo, museums here have a permanent exhibition of the best Latin American art and architecture throughout the South American continent. The contemporary profile of a half-dozen buildings of The Latin American Memorial Complex is full of Latin American art. This complex is easily accessible by subway, is clean and modern, one of the best in the world.

Do not miss the furniture dating from the imperial period in Brazil at the Ipiranga Imperial Museum (Museu Paulista). With so many resources and facilities, this city is a delight to experience and explore. The broad avenues of Avenida Paulista, the main street of St. Paul, are a great place to start exploring the city on foot.

Sao Paulo is a fascinating juxtaposition of old and new, here you can find colonial-immersed in the splendor of modern amenities. Sao Paulo is a city waiting to be discovered, clean, bright and exciting, this town is completely revolutionize your idea of Brazil.

BRASILIA
Brasilia was built by the country's leading architects, Oscar Niemeyer and Lucio Costa, in 1950 to replace Rio as the capital of Brazil. However, this does not mean that the design of the city has been well thought out. To be honest, Brasilia was intended as the administrative capital of Brazil, who is also a feature in recent days. However, the architects of the city had not considered the private construction companies existing in Brasilia. Accordingly, all the good intentions of the architects were lost and the city today is little more than a sprawling mess of buildings with modern design. All in all then, Brasilia definitely worth a visit if you have so much time!

MANAUS
Located in the heart of the Amazon Basin, Manaus is a popular destination for tourists looking for exotic excursions in the heart of the Amazon. Manaus offer two great attractions for its tourists. The first is obviously the opportunity to travel in the Amazon Basin, the second is the chance to see some of the largest ocean-going ships in the world entering the port until a thousand miles inland, where they load and unload products.

RECIFE
Located on the Gold Coast of Brazil (northeastern Brazil), Recife is a popular tourist destination. Recife is also known for the number of canals and bridges that cross the city, so also called the "Venice of Brazil". The city also has a number of museums and churches. However, no visit to Recife is complete without a visit to the old city jail, to make your visit even more interesting, now the complex also features a shopping mall.
Recife is the capital of Pernambuco state and is considered one of the most important seaports of Brazil. Recife is the fifth largest city in Brazil, but is less modern and cosmopolitan than some other large Brazilian cities. The Guarapares International Airport is the airport of the city and offers numerous flights to and from this destination. Recife was founded as a port city nestled

between white sandy beaches dotted with palm trees and coral reefs. The urban area is growing rapidly and is connected by a series of bridges and waterways. In 1982, the nearby city of Olinda was declared a UNESCO World Heritage and Tourism obviously has been affected positively.

Recife's name derives from the Portuguese word "recife de coral" in fact "reef". The area was one of the first in Brazil to rise from Portuguese rule in 1534. The state of Pernambuco prospered with sugar cane industry, which was originally introduced in the area by Duarte Coelho. Recife was a very fertile area with a climate suitable for growing sugar cane. The indigenous peoples of Brazil have been employed to work the land and cultivate sugar cane fields. When that was no longer a viable solution to produce, slaves were brought from Africa gathered in the country between the 16th century and 19th century to replace the indigenous population is not so cooperative and replaced for the work in the fields. The Brazilian keep very visible elements of black culture in food, dance and music because of the influence of the African people. The combination of Indians, slaves, blacks and Portuguese was so high that made Recife one of the most culturally diverse country.

The Carnival of Recife has a famous tradition and is one of the most beautiful and famous in Brazil.

Every hotel in Recife waits with open arms in this time of year. The streets come alive with native Indian and African Maracatu beats to Frevo and samba. You will be enchanted by the atmosphere, the sounds and the parades of the Carnival.

SAO LUIS

Sao Luis, which was named by King Louis XIII (of France), is considered one of the most beautiful cities in Brazil. The architecture of the colonial city and was founded by a French pirate, with magnificent churches and palaces. Sao Luis is nothing short of enchanting and is a delightful fusion of all the cultures of Brazil: African, indigenous and Portuguese. It is really worth to visit this beautiful town.

NATAL

Natal is the capital of Rio Grande Do Norte. E 'surrounded by beautiful beaches and sand dunes that run along its 40 kilometers of coastline. Geographically speaking Natal is the closest point of Brazil to Europe. Natal has two urban centers, including the cities of Ponta Negra and Natal, the latter is the most popular area for entertainment, restaurants and accommodation. Known as the "City of the Sun" and also "The City of Dune", Natal is located in the northeastern tip of Brazil. Located about 15 degrees south of the equator the sun shines for more than 3,000 hours each year. The average temperature in Natal is about 28 degrees Celsius. During the summer reaches 38 degrees Celsius.

When you plan a holiday in Natal keep in mind that the best time to visit is from November to February and again in July. There are four and five star hotels which are located along the "Via Costeira" which offer an excellent service. They are all directly facing the beach and most rooms have splendid views of the ocean. To find a wider range of accommodation is enough to move in Ponta Negra, where you can find a variety of hotels that meet the needs of every pocket. No holiday in Natal would be complete without a tour of the many beaches both north and south of Natal, definitely stands out among the most famous Pipa.

FORTALEZA

Two words define the state capital of Ceará: Sun and Day. Fortaleza is the Brazilian coastal city with most sunny days throughout the year. Fortaleza is a hot city with a pleasant breeze along the coast, with small changes in temperature during the year that Fortaleza is located very close to the equator. There is a slight drop in temperature from April to August, but the temperature remains between 24 and 28 degrees Celsius. The rest of the year the temperature is 30 degrees Celsius.

The "forro" music style is typical of the region in the north-east, is in the blood of the people and listen anywhere: on the beach, in bars, restaurants, clubs and streets of the city. Most of the bars and beaches are open until very late and some of the resorts as Canoa Quebrada Cumbuco and often do not close its remaining open until dawn and beyond.

The nightlife begins to stir around midnight and then goes on until the wee hours of the morning. The main tourist destinations are located on Iracema Beach with several nightclubs and bars such as Café del Mar and Mambo, and the "Pirate" the nightclub famous for its dedicated music lovers Monday Forrò.

Famous for its friendliness and hospitality of its people, for his animated lighting and an incredible cultural diversity, Fortaleza is a city well-developed and has modern facilities, ports, international airport, the best international hotel chains, shopping malls, theaters, bars, discos, as well as ample green and leisure areas. It was for decades a popular destination for Brazilian tourists, but in recent years, the fame of Fortaleza is coming to the world and the number of Europeans, North and South Americans coming in Ceara has grown rapidly.

The sea, which runs along the city, has a variety of attractions. The most important urban beaches of Fortaleza are Meireles, Volta and Jurema Mucuripe, connected by the Avenida Beira-Mar. There are modern buildings, including first-class hotels, numerous bars on the beach (barracas) and restaurants serving delicious local cuisine and dishes made with seafood. Praia do Futuro in the south east of the city is another popular tourist beach with its beautiful white sand and a relaxed atmosphere of about 7 km in length, is the favorite for swimming and surfing. Praia do Futuro has been made famous by his "barracas" (rustic restaurants built along the beach), which offer excellent local cuisine and musical shows. Ponta das Dunas Beach Park, just outside the city, is the largest water park in Brazil, and also offers one of the best hotel-resort in Brazil.

The beach of Cumbuco is famous for windsurfing and the exciting buggy rides on miles and miles of sand dunes. One of the many popular attractions in Cumbuco is the "Lagoa do Banana", where guests can enjoy many water activities such as kayaking, boat rides and banana-boat on the lagoon. Thanks to its attractions and its proximity to Fortaleza (30 minutes drive from the city), Cumbuco is one of the locations in Brazil with the increased presence of foreigners in search of a residence. This has caused a boom in real estate and construction.

Returning to the city of Fortaleza, the same is also celebrated for its culture and for keeping the architectural characteristics of the end of the century. Some major attractions are the buildings in Estoril, home to many restaurants and also an exhibition gallery. The Bridge "Dos Ingleses" (bridge of the English) and the Centro Cultural Dragão do Mar, one of the most advanced and comprehensive cultural centers of Brazil. Do not forget the Statue of Iracema, a symbol of the city.

Just like any city, even this is not 100% perfect, Fortaleza has many poor areas, including some favelas, and other hazardous areas within the city. So it should be always be careful, leave jewelry and valuables in the hotel, carry only the bare minimum in currency and not to go into the streets and places unknown.

CURITIBA

Curitiba is a city of 1.5 million inhabitants, many of them are European descent, and an important port. The city dates back to 1669, with the first European settlement and rubber plantations which led to the decline in wealth in 1920. Today the city is known for its imports of Brazil nuts, and electronic production equipment and oil refining.

The city of Curitiba has to care about the environment with an innovative urban planning with many parks and gardens. One of the best is the garden "Jardim Botanico", which includes a greenhouse in the shape of two-story castle. The Botanical Museum in the park has a wide range of exotic plants in Brazil.

One of the most popular attractions is the typical tourist train that travels between Curitiba and Paranagua. Completed in 1880, offers a breathtaking journey of three hours, traveling within 13 tunnels and crossing over 67 bridges. Along the way, you will see rivers, waterfalls and vibrant vegetation. One of the two trains a day is specifically for tourists. Especially handy with cars stopping in the most panoramic and charming. A regular train, at a much lower price, is also available.

FLORIANOPOLIS

Florianopolis, or Floripa as it is also known, is the state capital of Santa Catarina which is located in southern Brazil. It has a lively and colorful mix of the best that Brazil has to offer and is located between the city of Porto Alegre and Curitiba. Located in a rich agricultural expanse of the city is a commercial and cultural mecca. The metropolitan area of the island is home for over 821,000 people, while the island itself is home for over 400,000 people. Florianopolis is connected to the mainland by a bridge that allows easy access to the rest of Brazil and neighboring countries. The northern half of the island of Florianopolis is the most densely populated, while the south remains more isolated and less developed. With more than 100 white sand beaches Florianapolis attracts many South Americans a year. Both domestic and international flights arrive and depart from the international Herciliop Luz. The city is located about an hour's flight from Sao Paulo and two-hour flight from Rio de Janeiro and there are also daily flights to and from all major cities in Brazil.

Florianopolis has a wide choice of hotels, guest houses and bed and breakfast (inns). There are also campsites for the more adventurous traveler. For a touch of luxury oceanfront suites can also find on the beach. There are many activities to do on this sub-tropical island including gliding, kayaking, windsurfing, kite-surfing, nature walks etc ... The locals and tourists fill the restaurants and bars. At the public market in downtown live music can be heard daily. According to regular visitors of the island, the best time to visit is between March and April.

STOP IT! I RUN AWAY AND OPEN A LITTLE BAR ...

Who did not cry, at least once in his life, "Stop it! I run away and open a little bar on a Caribbean beach." And It's the leitmotif that marks the lives of stressed out and frustrated ones, who face daily many difficulties that modern society brings with it, jobs, taxes, traffic, children, the bureaucracy, the exasperated careerism, competition, smog, trash TV, the rampant dishonesty. There all the ingredients to going crazy, and how much! Surfing online in internet, searching on search engines such words as "flight from Italy" or "quality of life", opens an amazing world of blogs, forums, stories and experiences of those who, in order to take a leap towards a new life, they did it (or intend to do it).

MOVE IN BRAZIL IS JUST A DREAM? NO, TODAY IT IS A GOOD IDEA!

Many of us grew up with the idea that "to live in Brazil," "give up everything and open a beach bar" were only dreams ...
But are they still so today?
Begin again in a fantastic country which nature almost untouched, festive and cheerful, with enormous resources and beautiful women .. A country seven times larger than Europe, which still must give proof of its great potential ... Europe and the United States are in a crisis ... The future is already in Brazil! And while the economy of Western countries (Italy, Spain, Europe and the U.S.) goes through a black crisis, Brazil is the best emerging market in the world according Citibank, has paid his debt and it is now even become a creditor nation . The profitability of Brazilian industries is more than the U.S. ones, the Brazilian economy is growing exponentially, wages rise, employment is growing, even the discovery of a huge oil field put the Brazil I the same places of Saudi Arabia in terms of reserves.
And the same Economist published a headline: "Does God is Brazilian ...?"
Now everything changed, young people are prepared to accept challenges, they are enterprising and well-informed and with the internet you can get huge amounts of information and you can buy a ticket in minutes.
So today going to live in Brazil is not so difficult. Just put aside fears and if you are really convinced, take the step ...
It will be because of the current economic situation, which you can euphemistically call it "swinging". Or for the reduced purchasing power of wages. Or perhaps the soaring property prices. Or even for insignificant interest charged on bank deposits. The fact is that today is increasingly less

attractive to invest in so-called 'save-haven'.

The main thrust to leave arises from the shortage of economic growth that we have in Europe in terms of small capital. "We think about the professional tired, the pensioner who can not get to the end of the month, the couple "shouldered ", and so on and so forth, all looking for a place in the sun. If we think of rampant Islamic terrorism, the paranoia of the third world war, we know many people have a reason to reach distant destinations". In short, the motivation to take the plunge and go and live abroad, leaving the "mother", are numerous. The most varied. From an emotional point of view what drives this step is especially the desire for adventure, to escape the daily routine and to explore our fantasies, becoming citizens of the world.

It'seasy to take the first step: just pack your bags, put in your pocket credit card, a bit of money, passports and so on. Depending on the country things can be easy or difficult. The reality, however, is not always so rosy.

Why Brazil has become fashionable among our countrymen, even to start business ventures?

Brazil is a country that offers a great diversity of landscapes, fauna, flora, climates and micro-economies to suit all tastes. The cost of living is still quite low. Then there are the music and the warmth of the people. This makes Brazil a place where you want to live. Then there is the apparent ease that lets you open a business.
The big problem is the laziness and lack of information.

We are telling the truth that in southern Brazil for example certain problems, that are fairly common in the Northeast, do not occur, but why move to a copy, while "brasilianized", of Europe? The problem is that most investors do not only look for a business: look for a place in the sun in general, something in front of the sea or in tourist areas. But this is like putting the wolf in the mouth. Most of the nightclubs and restaurants in the tourist area pays protection authorities, and the sea front in theory does not permit anything. It seems that we want to discourage the big move to Brazil. Not so. But it's important to clarify that in Brazil, perhaps more than anywhere else, you need planning. Our advice is to search on the Internet on specialized sites, forums, discussion lists, but unfortunately there are many time wasters or people who feel experts. In any case, listen to various opinions never hurts. Not only in Brazil, but a little everywhere, expatriates have problems of integration. This is why Brazil Real Property, www.brazilrealproperty.com, already present in Brazil for 10 years, has published both this book and the guide "Investing in Brazil. What to do and what not to do ... " published in various languages and formats, E-book (electronic book) written by expatriates for future expatriates. The advantage of e-books is that you can continually update. The advantages that the largest South American country offers to people who wants to drop everything and start away from home a new economic activity are mainly: climate, a stable economy, protection of foreign investment, an easy language to learn and a culture similar to ours .

We recommend pensioners and all those who have capital of at least one hundred thousand euro (the law requires R $ 150,000 at today's exchange rate of approximately 69,000 euro to get residence visa through investment) that they pack their bags . With little money, the risk of losing everything is great. Obviously it depends on personal skills and how you want to live. If you are willing to live in a "favela" and eat rice and beans you will survive, but if you want to have a car, a house and decent food, then life is not so cheap. The car is considered a luxury item and gasoline costs the same as in Europe. Then there is the chapter of fines: go with the red light, so for example, can cost half a "minimum wage". In conclusion, the more people we recommend Brazil are retirees or those who can live on a pension. Here with a thousand euro per month we live pretty well, we can afford things that in Europe could not be done. Furthermore, the visas are for retirees easy to obtain.

Brazil is a paradise to live only to a pension or investment property. To work here you have to be professional and have a good dose of patience. We will divide real estate investments into three categories.
- In the short term, say one year, are good investments in the city, as property to be renovated or purchased in advance (on paper). Any capital, in this case, it is interesting.
- In the medium term ,two or three years, will be right for tou a pousada, which is a pension, or land "sea view", or subdivisions in the northeast.
- In the long term, between five and ten years, relying on properties in remote areas in general more distant than one hundred kilometers from an international airport or in the Amazon region. "

THE POUSADA

Every day that goes by the word "Pousada", similar to our Bred & breakfast, enters more and more frequently in common terminology. It 's easy in fact to run into the speeches of people who had the idea of opening a pousada in Brazil and discover the existence of an entirely new work (at least for us Europeans) and certainly profitable. But what is really a pousada? The alternative to a hotel for tourists are to rent a house (but at least one week) or to stay in some hostel at low prices, but such arrangements are usually not very suitable for tourists who planned a vacation a few days when you do not want to give up comfort and convenience that only could be found in a hotel. Thus was born the "pousada", the ideal solution for those on a small budget without sacrificing the quality of the hosting structure.

BREAKFAST / CAFE 'IN MANHA

In the management of the pousada breakfast time plays a particular important role. It's in this small period of time that the manager of the pousada offers the visitor's knowledge of the area by disseminating valuable information to reach the main tourist destinations.

Think it might be important for a tourist to know which direction to move without having to turn in vain and maybe find some kind of part of the city. In the early morning you have a way to become familiar with our guest who will be happy to tell you about their adventures during their holiday. We point out that the tourist who decides to stay in a pousada is a person who loves contact with people and is looking for new relationships.

Also remember that the image which the visitor will take of your lodging is not just the beauty of the rooms but also the relationships that you will be able to engage with him.

The time you steal from work is a time well spent, because you want to use it to achieve happiness and to devote yourself to passions.

Brazil Real Property

REAL TESTIMONIALS

Natal: Marco Moretto
My New Life in Rio Grande Do Norte

My name is Marco Moretto, I'm from Vicenza. I'm married to a Brazilian woman with a beautiful two year old son, I am an entrepreneur. I write from the city of Natal, in the north-eastern Brazilian coast. Natal is the state capital of Rio Grande do Norte and counts with 800,000 inhabitants. This is a rather famous place in the international tourist trail, for about 300 sunny days a year and a warm / windy climate with 28/30° Celsius. After having often go to this town for over ten years as a tourist with my wife Cynthia, a couple of years me and my family moved to this city with the aim of starting a new life path. I state that for many years intimately cherished the idea of an experience of living abroad, it always fascinated me and brought me to know about some countries; Brazil, among them, let me feel very comfortable the first time .
The work was good in recent years, with the growth of our employment increase in line with the commitments it then became a time effort, stress, dissatisfaction, a kind of large blender where both me and my wife found ourselves surrounded without seeing a way to mediate between the economic well-being and the quality of life.
This leads us to seek balance and then to dream of an alternative that culminated with the sale of the company.
At this point we were free from constraints working and we had a duty to do something for ourselves, we could dream, but also realize our dreams, a perfect condition.
Natal has been the obvious choice, since it's my wife native place and, consequently, the city I know best and wher we often go annually. Brazil is considered one of the emerging states, and economic / business indications that we had were in favor, then it was enough to think of a lot less stressful pace of life ... here we found our next destination.
Here with great enthusiasm we decided to found Bienova (www.bienova.com), a shop of 200 sqm. dedicated bathroom furnishings and located in the main shopping street of the city.
Bienova contains the meaning of our fundamental change in the composition of the word, the shop is ideally a tribute to our son Gabriel (diminutive Portuguese: BIEL) and our new life (NOVA), hence BIENOVA. With the pure

entrepreneurial spirit that characterizes the Venetians, we plunged fearlessly into this new experience and we are taking an interesting experience. After many months now, I can witness how the roots of my country are rooted in me, but above all how the teaching received at home can be an excellent base from which to assert ourselves and consider the world.

Q: What is the commonplaces further from the truth about Brazil?

I believe that in general the cliché handed down to us by the media about Brazil is relax and coconut palm: it is sold as "tropical dream." Often repeat that the tropical dream does not exist, it is a casting stress stereotype that moves the imagination of many of us and that often dazzles us, a kind of care for our moments of frustration. Here in Natal, just as in other countries, we must win it all with our own forces and indeed, if possible, because we foreigners have to pay the price to be included in a mindset that is not exactly the same in which we grew. If the cliché worked, the beaches would be full of kiosks operated by foreigners, all offering fruit-based spirits and surrounded by beautiful as the famous film by Tom Cruise - Cocktails & Dreams - remember?

Q: More and more people decide to leave Italy to pursue their dreams elsewhere. Whose responsibility?

I'm out of Italy since more than two years and then I was not overwhelmed by the tsunami of economic crisis, however, I feel that the dissatisfaction of those who can not see their efforts recognized is great.
Unfortunately, living in the capitalist system has price you pay: it makes us dream and desire, it goes on offering us things that we apparently can not give up, and creates the frustration of reaching something. When this do not happens the small personal tragedies and disappointments trigger. The Brazilian is able to be happy with small comforts, while we Europeans are not able to satisfy us.
I believe that eventually all the liability is attributable not to human being, but to the system in which we are involved, in the model.

Q: And you, when did you realize your dream you would have earned abroad?

The dream of being happier pervades all of us sooner or later, I still run after him.
In reality I have not so much certainties, I've not being here in Natal long time enough to understand, and I am going through the phase of acclimatization. Help of my wife is crucial, the inclusion being alone can be a little more difficult.

Q: Your secret place in Natal.

Here in Natal, the average temperature is 28 degrees all year round, and then the sun is king, this is already a good help for good humor. The pace of life is inevitably slowed down by weather and a certain inertia, and perhaps this can also be an education in certain situations, the climate is wonderful and there are apparently all the trappings to describe a beautiful novel of ideals and comfort.
Personally when I want a moment for me I dip in my pool, listening to the sounds of nature.
These are priceless feelings that are difficult to objectively found in Vicenza. When it is so we find ourselves truly in harmony with oneself.

Q: do you regret your choice?

Have don't regret my choice and I think it is a very constructive chance I would recommend to many people. My testimonial is intended to be an incentive for everyone to fight for his dream, as well as a morale boost to emphasize that you appreciate the beautiful city of Vicenza even more when you live far away.

Um Abraço a todos, and an invitation to dream again without ever give up ...

Marco Moretto

Cuiabá: Eugenio Ballarin
My New Life in Mato Grosso

Electrical engineer and manager in several multinational companies, after a reduction (almost total) of staff in my company and several months to send CVs around Europe without even an answer, I decided to go to Brazil. My girlfriend is of Cuiaba in Mato Grosso, and then we settled here. I like the place, because there are few tourists and Europeans and there are still many things to do.

Q: What is the common place further from the truth about Brazil?

The image of Brazil that we always see is that of Rio de Janeiro, or mulatto people dancing to the rhythm of Samba. Questionable in many ways, Brazil you listen more to Forrò and Sertaneja (sort of "Country Brasilian music) than to Samba, is much more common to see that mestizos than mulatos. Finally, there is a lot of people who are absolutely hostile to the carnival culture. In Mato Grosso the religious-moralistic Evangelical background is very strong, it reminds me of the Southern Baptist United States, where almost all believers are as vehement, though often the behavior is not as immaculate. The stereotype of the Brazilian as a little careless person, however, is quite well chosen, they are excellent companions for holiday, but if they are business associates, or worse, suppliers, they quickly become very unfriendly. An advice? Never pay in advance, or at least the minimum possible! Need to do with a bit of a reason, otherwise you go insane. When I fix an appointment for 11:59 noon, they ask me why perplexed, then I tell them I'm leaving at noon o'clock. Then you have to smile when they arrive with half an hour late (if it fits)! What bothers some people is that they do not phone when they decide not to move at all. For a European this seems disrespectful, but for a Brazilian, or at least many, it is perfectly normal, however they do not do so with evil.

Q: do you regret your choice?

Not for now, but I'm here since one year, perhaps early to evaluate. Brazil is not only romance, there's a lot of violence carefree, and many Italians flaws here are so blatant (corruption, bureaucracy). However I miss only my Italian friends, but here is a so beautiful climate, sunshine, happiness and economic growth that in short it seems to me that the future is better here.

Eugenio Ballarin

Maceió: Mauro Alvisi
My New Life in Alagoas

My name is Mauro Alvisi, I've been living for more than 6 years in a beautiful city in North East Brazil, Maceio, the capital of the state of Alagoas (lagoons), it takes its name from the fact that it is full of beautiful lagoons. I live a few miles outside the city, near the beach, in a village populated mostly by fishermen, a quiet resort, but only 10 minutes from the city.
Wondering why I radically changed my life and I moved here? Well usually jokingly I say I do not know in truth, there is not only one reason, but several. Let's step back a little, 7 years ago, in Easter 2003 period, about three weeks before I left for Thailand, an outbreak of SARS.
On TV all were on alert with masks, my friend D. called me and told me that he had decided not to leave, the first thought in my hot head was "What a pity, I will miss, but I go by myself". Then I thought: my English is poor and tending to the poorest, they also speak bad english there, so why I go there alone, half a world away in a place where there is an epidemic? So we set another goal, and since I had already been in some places in Brazil we ask the agency to change, I did not know Maceio, but I had heard about it and I was teased, then we included Maceio among the possible destinations. They found only one flight... to Maceio and then ... we start, me understanding two words and spoking one of Portuguese language, and D. that he understood and spoke a single one.
We arrive at the airport and take a taxi in the direction of the city to look for

accommodation here ... this weird feeling started there... I remember as if it were now on the way I began to feel a strange and pleasant euphoria that climbed from the belly up neck and could not understand what it was, I looked back and did not understand in fact, the road that leads from the airport into town is not at all nice, but ... this strange and nice feeling was getting stronger, every time I turned around to D. and looked at him with a smile from ear to ear, and he did not understand what I have to be so happy, yes ok, we were on vacation, but after a tiring trip and the hassle of having still to find a hotel somewhere we did not know and with some difficult communication, all this happiness had no sense ... in short, the vacation was wonderful and we returned in August, I was always more in love with the place and a few days before returning with the help of some Italians who had known and lived there for some time, I bought a house outside the city, near the beach, a house to replace because it was dirty and shabby, but my friend E. worked hard and let the house become a little flower. I must admit that despite my "gambling" and my inexplicable haste, I was very lucky, I found serious and honest people, both Brazilians and Italians, and then, when I went back, the house was ready and documents in place.

I do not recommend to anyone a lightness like mine, in fact, as in all places in the world, the nasty surprises may be just around the corner and come from the natives, but often by his countrymen, so it is good practice to get a good lawyer or someone who has experience and know how to get around the place.

The just had bought the house,(August 2003) so I went back to Italy very euphoric, my thought was, 'well, now in a couple of years I put things right then I move', but why leave Italy? You ask, it's so bad? NO, it was very well, "almost everything", I had a very good job (but I did not like most) that allowed me very flexible hours, a certain prestige, and that made me make good money! I lived in a beautiful villa, which filled with every kind of comfort, there was everything I liked, giant plasma, fireplace, cherry parquet, air conditioning in all rooms and the music everywhere, including the bathroom, where there was a Jacuzzi hydromassage and turkish bath, in fact I had done my size and taste, and was placed on the hills of Bologna, ear Monteveglio, in a little village with few cars, located in between two hills and with a small river in front, I loved being in the green and quiet, I remember summer nights there were fireflies, not seen since I was a child.

In the afternoon when it was summer I did some great motorcycle rides, I "almost" all that I wanted, but then why go? Well, you remember that "almost everything"?

For a while I did not feel more satisfied, I began to see the faces increasingly sad, dejected, and angry people (probably for the continuing fiscal pressures and moral issues, let us tell the truth in our beautiful country, the population is increasingly " juice "and then, you can not do anything!, everything is forbidden!), lacked the brightness in their faces and I felt increasingly" uncomfortable ", my job did not give me more stimulation and if I continued I would not have done with seriousness and dedication, "I did not like anymore."

Since 1997, however I was passionate about alternative therapies, and continued my studies in all areas that gave me a positive vibration so I have very spaced, Reiki, kinesiology, reflexology, massage, Bach flower, and now EFT (Emotional Freedom Technique) but I was not making the best of my knowledge in the field and at that time I did not know if I would have never made a profession, I felt closer and closer and I wanted to get away, my thought was to put me a looong 'holiday period' and it became stronger every day, I saw a dear friend of mine complaining, he was and is still doing a job he hates, he is also poorly paid, with the mirage of a pension, (minor) but every time it came closer, bummm, those who "squeeze the people" nicely kick him back a few years and so he has come at my age, sad and angry, with empty hands and still does the job he hates, and then I thought, know what is it? I'm going! So I burn up the track, I organized myself, but this time considering all the pros and cons, I did well the accounts, I was single and without children, my mother lived with my sister and both enjoyed excellent health, I also evaluated the possibility that it was only a mirage and that after a few months, woke up, could not enjoy being in that place, so I resigned and on February 2004, 2nd, I started with a one-way flight without knowing clearly what I would done in the future, but still keeping my house, my car and a nest egg in case I would go back. I clearly remember my Head and still a good friend L. concerned with me on the phone 'but why? What happened? Want to see your position? but you go to work for the competition?' At one point I had to just tell him: NO, YOU DON'T UNDERSTAND! I'm leaving! GO TO LIVE IN BRAziiiiiiL!

That news sparked considerable confusion and disbelief among all friends, relatives and acquaintances, wondering why I were behaving so madly, is perhaps to escape from the authorities? Did he cheat someone? the questions were 'what will you do? What will you eat? and delinquency? and prostitution?' Well, I did not know what to say apart 'a long vacation', but I must say that these questions made me realize how little we know and how many assumptions are above the country, speaking of the state where I live, that compared to the south of Brazil still has to grow, I must say that there is very little information and very often distorted, but please .... What do you eat?? Apart from the fact that I personally appreciate the delicious local cuisine, as a true Italian I still keep most of the time a diet rich in fruits and vegetables, seafood pasta, prepared in our own way and here is everything, pasta, cheese, ham, olive oil etc. ... some of these products are excellent and others mediocre, but I am a lover of fish and the fishermen bring me fresh fish and lobster (15 reais per kg today about 7 € ... need I say more?)when they come back, not to mention the fruits that are delicious. To say the least, in short, diet is far from being a problem, rather it is a great pleasure, but I remember that I replied to one of those such as "know it alls" that I would have lived in a hut and I would have fed on berries and roots ... what a laugh I'm done.

Crime? Always talking about the city where I live, there is, as in almost all places in the world, personally I consider it still a pretty quiet place, apart from some areas, you can stroll along the seafront until later without too much trouble, it is clear that if you go to the search for late night in a favela or shady places, you will find trouble, then I act wisely as I did in Italy, I avoid some places as I avoided too (without naming names) some slums of our Italian cities.

And the prostitutes? well, it happens, they are also here, but I must say that (in the city where I live) on the street there are only some of them, almost not seen, but which can not be said of the old town Bologna, where are plenty of them on the avenues at night and in daylight.
Thus dispelling these commonplaces and not worrying about all those who in some way told me "I wanted your own good", I went, on December 2004 the 2nd I moved; think of a person who goes from -5° to 30°, in a place near the sea where the sun shines 10 months a year and the other 2 months, it rains a lot, but not continuously, and when the sun comes out is 28/29 C°...then?!! The first months were a total joy, imagine a house 40 mt. far from the beach, with almost 1000 square meters of garden and a pool of 50 sq. m., my friend E. also had the whirlpool tub (outdoors of course) and because he didn't find one as big as I wanted, he made one using a children pool, has the same effect, but 6 people can go in it, not bad, right? Life flowed delicious, no worries, served and revered like a pasha, I left a nice place for an even better one and I was just fine, two months later I decided to buy two dogs, I had always loved cats, but this time there was the space and the condition of keeping large dogs, then when I was looking for two female Doberman, I found two sisters of 60 days born Feb. 2nd, the same day I arrived in Brazil. I take home these two delicious pets and I call them Gina and EMI, the first as the friendly film actress, and the second as a Spanish friend of mine, very sweet, and after some time they begin walking on the beach, how wonderful, I got up when I wanted , wonderful breakfast on the veranda and then go, to sea, walks, visiting new places, and in the evening we went out to dinner and then enjoy a free ride, I spent time doing this kind of shameful life, my

sabbatical year was prolonged and I thought that I never got tired of living like this, but because of a small empty space inside of me and my genetics that always pushes me to do and to be useful in some way, I said that I was not here just for that.

Some time later, one day I was in Praia do Frances in the restaurant of a friend, and between a spaghetti with shrimp and a glass of wine he speaks to me of a neighbor, an American who was carrying out a project for a school for poor children, while M. talked about feeling a pleasant feeling, this thing attracted   me.

I set a meeting, I liked Q. immediately, with that angelic and honest face, he spoke in a calm and relaxed tone and when I asked him what it was called the project he said Starfish, starfish, that was the signal for me. Some years ago, when I was still studying kinesiology, a person whom I respect very much, very significant, sent me a story, with an invitation to make   a   difference,   I   remember   it   affected   me   deeply. I summarize briefly.

"One morning after a heavy storm, a wise man who used to walk on the beach before he starts writing, he saw a human figure in the distance that seemed to dance, he smiled at the thought that someone was dancing to celebrate the the sunrise, and he quickened his pace to reach that person, getting closer he realized that he was a kid and that he was picking up something from the sand and gently throwing it back into the sea, and then the man asked: "What are you doing?" The boy replied, "I'm throwing the stars back into the sea, otherwise they will die." The wise man said, "but they are thousands, you see? You won't be able to save them all." The boy looked at him and threw back another star into the sea, then he said "It is true, I can not save them all, but each one that I will save, it will make a difference for her and for the world."

The project of D. was very important and far-sighted, to bring children up to the age where they could either continue to study or learn a job and also follow this step, involving parents with handicrafts to support themselves and help the school, everything was taken care of, in particular diet even had a special care in terms of balance and types of products (if you want, the details are on the site of the school http://www.escolaestreladomar.org/home/it.html), so I decided to support it .

My commitment was to find funds from Italy.

The start took place in a very poor neighborhood and a very old house, when D.,at that time not yet married, was going back to the U.S. and I followed things up a little more closely.

There were many difficulties and not just to recover the funds, I think it was a rumor that D. was going to sell the organs of children, the life experience of those people prevented them from accepting the fact that there was someone who would do this only to help others and not for profit or otherwise, (actually something like this it's not every day) also the associations so-called "beneficial"were barriers that never fails to put a spoke in the wheel, I remember the discomfort, I did not understand the reason for this hostility, even the attitudes of children parents were not helping, and the staff, even though they knew that D. was doing this just to give those children a better future using his own resources, never fails to find sneaky ways to try to extort money from him.

I must admit, D. and his wife C. had an extraordinary patience and dedication, one year after the site changed, moved into a house with a smaller garden, but the structure was broader and stronger, it housed 23 children, my job gave him some fruit but not what we expected and I was beginning to lose heart, when one day, a friend told me that a friend of him had a friend who would come every other day, unfortunately this lady had recently lost her son in a plane crash and wanted to realize her son project that was precisely to create a framework to help the poor children of Brazil.

While my friend was speaking I felt that feeling again and I thought "that's it", I asked him to arrange a meeting as soon as possible, to be the first, since he would consider other possibilities, so I dusted off some old techniques and with all the good intentions of world, I prepared myself, I got all what I wanted to say, to do, and the final goal.

On the evening of the meeting I made sure to sit next to her and I started my job.

I must admit that at that time I have used some form of communication that can be considered slightly manipulative, to tip the scales in favor of our children, but now I do not regret, in fact I did not tell any lies and didn't omitted any truth, the project was clear and very transparent sounded and the people who promoted it were honest and trustworthy.

After a few days and after considering other possibilities this lady told us that she would support the project, and would give the association the name of the child.

Thanks to this person and her desire for a child, but also to D. and C. who have looked after it and pampered as a child, the school now is very important, is home for over 120 children and is growing. Take a tour of the site will give you the feeling of breathing fresh air in the pollution of our days. Today, I follow it from afar, but it was a very important stage of my life. Taking a step back to the early days of the school, one day D. asked me if I could help some children with Bach flowers and show the teachers some techniques that could be applied to the children.

That request immediately gave me new life and I immediately started work, he had awakened something that had been sleeping inside of me. I began again to study the texts but also to do further research and experiment with new techniques, a few months later decided to open a studio where I worked with alternative therapies.

I soon realized that nobody knew the kinesiology and all people looked from a distance, some with some mistrust and others with some interest, it provoked interest, I was invited by some local TV and radio to explain my work. Most of the people who called me wanted to know if this type of therapy had an arrangement with the health insurances, customers who I had were selected and were of a very high cultural level, but not enough to cover the cost of a rent, a secretary, and the bills to reward my work.

I was invited to collaborate with some health centers, I remember a doctor who was showing me the structure quite finished, she asked me what it was. And when I began to explain that embraces many techniques and works with virtually all muscles, neurolymphatic, neurovascular, diet, flowers, and more she lost her smile, raised her arms to his chest in a clear sign of closure and said, okay OK, then I will get in touch ... She never called me again.

I had so much work to use my time looking for new things, one day I found an article on 'EFT (Emotional Freedom Technique) it came from TFT, such a technique that works on the meridians of acupuncture, but without the need for needles, I had studied it on the surface years earlier, but it was much improved and simplified after, I went headlong into this news, I began to use it with excellent results and the fact that it can be self applied and can be done remotely, with virtually the same results, considering the fact that staying in Maceió I can help a person living anywhere in the world, provided that he has a phone or internet, the advantage is great, then I closed the study and then go to another site and now I work well with the comfort of my home on appointment and without the payment of rent, secretary, billing, transport etc ... much better right?

Later maybe I will start to make some progress, to spread better and give people the opportunity to learn.

And decided to write an e-book on alternative therapies. The goal was and is to help people achieve a good mental and physical balance and then maintain it, after several days the translator and the technician that created the site and supervised the layout and images appeared, then the concern in me that little was left disappeared.

The help of E. (the web designer of the site) has been fundamental, I also gave some very interesting ideas such as taking and including small movies (home made, taken in my backyard) to show the points and how to stimulate them. I should say that E. has done a great job.

Now, the e-book is for sale online, still not very visible, but with passing of time it will get surely good results. http://www.ebooksaudeebemestar.com.br/. Oh, I forget, I also threw myself in the building industry.

Summer 2008, big lunch in a friend's house, in Praia do Frances, what with a barbecue, a caipiroska and a dip in the pool, we enter the speech on how was good there, that the subdivision was beautiful, the town was growing, that the building plots were still cheap, so euphoria of the moment took me and I asked him if he could find one plot there for me. So maybe later I would have built a house also in that location.

I do not remember what I said, I was tipsy, however several days later he called me and told me that there was a land available next to his house, the fumes of alcohol had passed but still it seemed a good idea, I took some time to think about it because I had a lot of irons in the fire, a house adjacent to that where I was living that I bought years ago and rented to tourists, and besides that the management of a villa of some friends who long ago decided making an investment, those colleagues of job and friends, remember? Well just them...

It seemed to me a lot of things, so I gave up ... for that week. In fact shortly after I bought two adjoining land, intending to use them something later. With the passage of time I had no longer the idea to build a house but some apartments, I thought, I would realize a small residence with 12 apartments with a pool in the middle of them.

I wanted to do it, but I did not understand anything about construction... A few days later I met my friend M, with the restaurant on the beach, he had already built a pousada and even a small residence like the one I wanted to do and since it is a serious person and I trust him I gave him the management of the site , well ... you know that it was not easy to work on staff, there was constant monitoring to avoid ambushes sleeping in the various corners, sometimes I was smiling because they reminded me of when I was 19 and worked in the workshop mechanics, I was out all night carousing and the day I fell asleep standing up, I went in the boxes of parts to crush a nap... and watch how roles change in life.

Today they are almost finished and they also came well, I'm moving to start selling them, I keep one for myself and sell others them or maybe I will sell someone and rent them to other people still waiting for they increase in value, I'll see ... For info on my property:

 http://www.brazilrealproperty.com/viewad.asp?id=50004980714100043

What will I do next? I do not know, maybe ... I relax, maybe ... This was my career in this country till today. Not bad for someone who wanted to go only on holiday? Yeah I know what you think ... " you went there to feel comfortable and then see how much you work!" In fact, standing here stimulates creativity and gives me energy to do, and I'm still haven't lose the habit to enjoy myself, where I live it's warm almost all year and we know that good weather will draw great benefits for the mood and the body. Since then every year I make a jump to Italy, the strange thing is that it is a burden for me to go, but people do not believe so, I prefer to spend the winter here rather than the summer there, I make a trip to visit my mother and my sister, but I remain the bare minimum 15/17 days, I even do a schedule of things to do in order to calculate the days, think that when I arrive in Portugal the boxes already run, and when I land in Bologna I began to feel uncomfortable.

There are also good times, it's clear, but after seeing that relatives and friends are well-being and after eating the noodles and tortellini that Mom makes, I want to go home.

All in all it's a good thing that I really like staying in Brazil,it means I made the right choice.

Sometimes I even meet someone with significant economic opportunities that tells me the usual phrase, "sooner or later I'm moving, but now I can not because blah blah blah", these people will remain on the doorstep all the life and some of them let slide without living it, and it is a sin. If you have the opportunities and conditions, do not do like me, I lost time, I waited up to 45 years!

Mauro Alvisi

Fortaleza / Natal / Recife: Stefano Marchese
My New Life in Rio Grande Do Norte

My name is Stefano Marchese and I am a businessman from Rome. I attend Brazil from 3 years and I lived there permanently for a year and a half, more specifically in the northeast of the country, divided between the towns of Praia Da Pipa (natural paradise situated 80km. in the south of Natal, where I managed a pousada for about a year) and the cities of Recife and Fortaleza. My contact with Brazil was random, based on the fairy tales of my friends, at the time I was still running a business in Rome, intrigued by the apparent ease and profitability of investments in that country, I accompanied one of them to verify personnally. My job at that time did not allow me to stay too long, but in just five days I got the enthusiasm, then I decided to buy an apartment (in a residential neighborhood in Recife). He returned to Rome I contacted an Italian lawyer via the Brazilian embassy, he lived in Fortaleza and through its local contacts he had a title search and real estate unit of the building, then I reassure myself of the validity of the deal. It was the first in a series of other real estate investment: a little later I opened a real estate company with three other Italian investors in order to better manage our property.

Q: What is the commonplace further from the truth about Brazil? The fact that everything is simple and profitable ... Despite the relative ease and convenience of my first impromptu investment then I had to suffer little to get income from it, through an endless series of scams by people apparently trust (girlfriends, real estate agents, brokers, artisans, tenants, etc ...) and still having already previously shunned people now proved to be unreliable, I say this not to discourage possible investors but rather to encourage them to arm themselves with patience and caution, after this you can make even the substantial business with healthy realism and choosing the right contacts ...

Q: More and more people decide to leave Italy to pursue their dreams elsewhere. Whose responsibility?

We should open a very large chapter that probably would take much space in this book ... Unfortunately we are pawns in a game of geopolitical strategies in which the lucky ones – also if only for adventurous spirit - try to position themselves in the few areas still left open to hope and personal ambition.

Q: And you, when did you realize your dream of earning abroad?

I always had the great fortune, or perhaps the wisdom to leave the boat just before it sank, whatever is the activity identified with this metaphor from time to time, ... a few years ago I had identified the increasingly disturbing signs of the next crisis to come and that it would irreparably undermined, without a swift reaction, the investments made in 10 hard years of sacrifice in the trade and, I think, tricky raids in property ... so in 2008 I could sell my business and, despite losing a lot of money, having to make an attractive redemption price, I managed to break free and to devote myself to the new adventure.

Q: Your secret place ....

Unfortunately I have never had much time to stop and enjoy the Brazilian pousada, also the subject of desire for many of our forebears, brought with all its imaginative iconography has proved anything but profitable and light activity: Brazil country has become a highly competitive and professionalism and quality have become the must-have, especially for us foreigners that we must excel compared to Brazilian inevitably enhanced by the "home turf" ... I admit that a key role in alleviating the country's effort to understand a seemingly easy to interpret were women, custodians of sensuality and femininity out of the ordinary: just a lewd caress, a Brazilian who also generously dispenses to a stranger as a refrain in a casual conversation, to make everything appear much more cheerful and pleasant

Q: do you regretted your choice?

No. I bitterly lament the fact that I can not build my own well-being in our homeland and I should also look with disdain turn towards more comfortable continents ... On the other hand, the alternative would have been investing in other emerging countries such as India, China or Russia, but the cultural proximity, favorable climate and ... why not admit it, because the women have made a difference in steering unmatched choice.

Stefano Marchese

MAKE MONEY IN BRAZIL WITH ICE CREAM

Loris & Loretta propose a successful investment here in Brazil. "Are you looking for an opportunity to invest abroad, or would you like to earn a business by an already proven and simple activity, would you like to go away from your country, but you do not know what activities to undertake? With our experience in the field of Ice Cream, we can help those who really want to change their lives. In the best course."

Our small firm "GIA" (homemade Italian ice cream), was born the idea of creating a structure able to export our experience in the manufacture of ice cream.

It's acceptable to all, young and old, because it is tasty, fresh and smooth. It melts in your mouth, and tickle the palate and leaves a pleasant feeling of relief. Ice cream is a genuine food, nutrient and not hypercaloric at all, as many might think. Dieticians and nutritionists are also very pleased with the part in weight loss diets, because the ice cream is a nice reward at the end of a lunch-controlled regime, a delicacy to be enjoyed as a snack or dessert, a wonderful opportunity as a substitute for a meal.

Our company is not a "franchising", requiring the customer to binding contracts, but rather an agency that allows the custome the complete freedom to develop the job as you like. We are an Italian couple living in Portugal "Algarve", for almost ten years. Here we opened a business, the production of ice cream (Italian), namely a laboratory where we manufacture the ice cream, and sell it to hotels, restaurants and ice cream parlors in the area.

Our current idea is to give the possibility to anyone who wants to undertake this activity, anywhere in the world.

Who sees it as a bomb of calories is wrong, indeed one might almost say that it is a product that can be considered a dietary ... Among the desserts, it has even fewer calories and less fat. From the standpoint of the nutritional properties, the cream is the best, fruit ice cream is rather less calories but low in most proteins (not used the egg yolk in preparing) and fat (often the milk is replaced by a fruit smoothie). With the same amount, the calories provided by the ice cream are 208 against 138 of the fruit.

If you want to reduce calories without giving up ice cream, choose hand-built (contain less concentrate fat than the industry), or soy-based yogurt only, or low-fat products, fat-free and with a small amount of sugar. The ice cream is not only good, but it is a valuable source of energy for our body. The fibers are the only substances that are completely missing.

According to their statistics, world population is greedy of ice cream, only in

Italy there are more than 33 million consumers, with sales of 4 billion euro every year and 600,000 tonnes of product sold 1,479,001,944 portions. The world record pro-capite! But as well as making extensive use, we are good in making it (do not forget, after all, we have created us in Florence in '500). In the U.S., for example, 10% of milk production is used for the production of ice cream. The 5 biggest consumers of ice cream in the world are: USA, New Zealand, Denmark, Australia, Belgium-Luxembourg.
World consumption has increased by 21% over the last 5 years and new markets are expanding in Asia, Africa and Latin America. the world's consumption of ice cream in liters per capita is:

New Zealand	22-23
U.S.	24
Australia	18
Finland	14
Ireland	13
Sweden	11.9
Canada	8.7
Italy	9.2
Denmark	8.7
United-Kingdom	8
Chile	5.6
Spain	5
Malaysia	2
China	1.9
Japan	0.01

With our experience in this field, we can help those who want to change the country and work. We can follow step by step the future ice cream makers, the choice of where to install the lab, purchase equipment necessary for the production of ice cream, purchase of raw materials and everything relating to the ice cream: school recipes (even those special tastes that we created specifically for the chef de cuisine) and opening several stores in order to allow even inexperienced people to build and maintain always and everywhere the standard of quality that has always distinguished the Italian ice cream in the world. Just recently, a simple laboratory in order to become the true masters of their own lives and their time. Where to open: mainly in countries with a strong annually tourism development, or in large cities with high population density, where there is a good number of hotels and restaurants of upper middle class. What you need: a room of approx. 45 sq m. and a minimum investment of €

45-50 thousand.

What we offer: assistance in project implementation.

Training of staff on site, both for the production of ice cream for marketing. Flanking both before and after the opening of the laboratory. "

For information contact:
Loris & Lorella
Mobile 00351 960-396289
Mail: loryelori@hotmail.com
http://www.ilgelatoitalianoartigianale.com

XII CENTURY WILL BE THE CENTURY OF BRAZIL

In early 2009 many economists argued that Brazil, along with other emerging markets would suffer a serious economic crisis that the world was going through. A year later, the situation is much different than they expected and the outlook for 2010 are clear: Brazil is one of the countries to join later in the crisis and one of the first to leave. For this reason the recovery of the Brazilian economy, been evident since mid-2009, is set to continue this year: in 2010 the government in Brasilia expects growth of 5% of GDP. The economic performance of the Lula government will also have major consequences on the political situation in Brazil, these performances, in fact, will only affect the outcome of federal elections to be held in October. For many heads of the First World he is the Man of the Year and one of the most influential people on the planet. As the Chilean colleague Michelle Bachelet he will leave power at the height of popularity and, like her, he is not seeking re-election obsession of many Latin American presidents. El Mundo has an interview Luiz Inacio Lula da Silva and basically it's nice to end the year with the union's first president of Brazil. Who wants to read the interview in the original language here:

http://www.elmundo.es/america/2009/12/29/brasil/1262057660.html

The Brazilians used to say that their country was "the country of the future", but a distant future ... I think that finally arrived?

I am convinced that the twenty-first century is the century in Brazil. We live in an exceptional time. Despite the crisis, we created this year more than 1.4 million jobs, while a million jobs have been sacrificed in rich countries. Also, investments have started to grow vigorously and in all sectors of the economy breathes optimism and confidence. We have won the democratic stability for the soundness of the institutions and respect for civil liberties and we are winning the biggest of our challenges: reducing poverty and social inequality.

His government managed to reduce poverty, it is a fact. An old Chinese proverb says, "Give a man a fish and you feed him for a day, teach him to fish and you feed him for the rest of his life." Do you think you made welfarism for removing poverty from people who can rely on themselves when they will end aid programs? Nice fish or fishing rods?

It's a popular saying also in Brazil. For this we are not giving away anything. What we are doing is helping people help themselves. Families receive assistance only if all school children are performing well and the family receives medical attention. With this we make sure that the next generation of Brazilians will have all the conditions to contribute productively to society, no longer being a prisoner of poverty or welfarism, that the only thing that gets played is poverty.

This year we saw a police helicopter shot down by gangsters in Rio de Janeiro. It is not the drugs the great enemy of democracy in Latin America? What your government did? It 's a problem that can be addressed by any country or would require coordinated political action among the various countries affected by the same problem?

As part of UNASUR you are creating a board dedicated to combating drug trafficking. Part of the solution of this complex problem is the reduction of poverty and inequality. Another part is the creation of educational opportunities for all.

In addition to the rhetoric, are something the leaders of the countries of Latin America? I cite a concrete result.
The top regional opportunities, especially because the leaders get a dialogue and build mutual trust. Its practical results are patented in the consolidation of regional integration with Mercosur and the increase in regional trade. More recently, the UNASUR has already demonstrated its value through effective action to reduce the threat to Bolivian stability in a time of great political tension.

He caused surprise to see her receive the president of Iran, a dictator whose election victory was challenged and who bloodily suppressed the opposition. It is surprising that someone who has fought against a dictatorship should bow to this. What do you say?
Iran's President Mahmoud Ahmadinejad presented himself for election and won 62% of the vote. Despite the discussions of the opposition, the elections were celebrated within the rules where there is vulnerable is the country's constitution. We have a commercial relationship with Iran dense and do not believe that putting him against the wall to attract the good causes. E 'need to create a space for dialogue and conversation, not to provoke a counter reaction.

Brazil has worked hard in the crisis in Honduras and little or nothing in the tension between Colombia and Venezuela. Why? Viewed with the perspective of time, it was a mistake to grant asylum in the Brazilian President Zelaya?
In the case of Colombia and Venezuela, Brazil has developed at different levels, including the UNASUR, a moderate attitude and has come to propose a monitoring scheme of the border, with the cooperation of Spain. As for the coup against President Zelaya, the Brazilian position has been clear, in keeping with our tradition and diplomatic events of the international community, there is no place for coups in Latin America.

The candidate and his minister Dilma Rousseff has no charisma. Do you think this is likely to affect the elections next October?
I see the electoral prospects with optimism. We have a candidate of great quality, who knows the government very well and has a great social sensitivity, great leadership skills and management of public machine.

REAL HAS BOOM, EURO TO PEAK

Real, who yesterday was quoted at € 2.29, after touching 2.19 also share has reached its historic high on the European currency, which in recent weeks and sank under the blows of the Brazilian currency. Therefore remain only a memory quotes around 3.40 (with a peak of 3.43) that were recorded at the end of 2008, the international financial crisis.

What are the reasons of the phenomenon? While the split of the Old Continent 'is certainly the most difficult period since it was created "in the words of German Chancellor Angela Merkel, because "the high deficit of Greece and the loss of credibility", exports and green-gold imports in the last month, showed the record ever for the month of February. The manager of the Ministry of Development Welber Barral remarked that the increase did not occur only in respect of 2009 - year notes marked by financial turmoil - but compared to 2008, "that was an exceptional year." The increase has mainly affected imports, grew by 50.8 percent compared to February 2009, while exports over the same period has increased by 27.2. Barral went on to explain that in Brazil there is a close correlation between imports and exports, with the first ones that tend to rise whenever there is an increase in the latter.

THE STOCK MARKET OF ST PAUL FIRST IN THE WORLD FOR GROWTH

In a time when all countries show a serious crisis the industry and the Brazilian stock market are rising fast   (ANSA) - SAO PAULO, Oct 27 - The Stock Exchange of São Paulo (BM & F Bovespa) recorded in the last twelve months, an increase of 121% real and 188% in dollar terms, the more high in the world after the global crisis .

The Bovespa index was down to 29,435 points on October 27, 2008, as a result of the explosion of the global crisis, and it 'arrived today at 65,470 points. The market value of the 443 companies listed on the Bovespa was 1.1 billion reais (about 440 million euro), and e 'arrived today 2.3 billion reais. Most of the shares 'strong in St. Paul, the mining company MMX and' climb of 473%, 178% Banco do Brasil, Petrobras 115% and 111% Vale do Rio Doce. Commodities such as oil and minerals have the lion's share in the Bovespa: Petrobras alone accounting for 18% of the total value. Compared to 188% of Sao Paulo, the Bombay Stock Exchange and 'Up by 119% to 105% of Hong Kong, one of Citta' in Mexico 82% and 81% in Shanghai. The Frankfurt Stock Exchange has regained 53% London 40%, the Dow Jones 20% and the

Nasdaq 42%. According to observers, the reasons for the boom of the Bovespa is the strong entry of foreign capital in Brazil, the architecture proved very strong during the macroeconomic crisis, the industrial park very diversified natural resources among the largest in the world and a good level of services.
SOURCE (ANSA)

Recession / crisis? In emerging is not heard. In Italy one out of two is pessimistic
Finally asleep! Yes, because with the economic crisis, as experts say the most important international organizations such as OECD and IMF, now behind consumers around the world can go back to peaceful sleep. According to the Doxa, in fact, who has just released the results of a study group Win (Worldwide Independent Network of Market Research), conducted in 22 countries around the world who monitored the perception of the population compared to the current economic crisis, at least one in two respondents (54%) suffered at least one of these four psychological disorders (considered as a direct result of the recession): sleep disturbance (26%), anxiety (40%), depression (18%) and stress (40%). And there have been more seriously affected the citizens of Japan, Russia, Lebanon, the U.S. and Mexico and to a lesser extent the population of the Netherlands, Austria, Italy, Spain and Brazil.
The research examines the different economic sectors touched by the crisis (personal income, real estate, the stability of banks and the stock market, cut costs, trust in government) and investigates the psychological effects produced by it in public. In general, the research shows that Brazil, Canada and India are the countries that are less affected by the crisis, where the level of optimism is higher than the average and also cuts the costs and the psychological consequences are more content. The most affected are France, Japan, Mexico, Argentina and Iceland.
As for the future, the survey shows that consumers are slowly regaining confidence in the financial conditions of their country and that the level of pessimism is considerably less than the previous survey conducted in March 2009. Almost half (45%) of respondents believe that the economic situation will remain unchanged over the next three months, while 19% think that will improve and 31% that will get worse. It also increases confidence in the stability and soundness of the stock market. With regard to fuel economy, at

least one in two (54%) say they have cut costs (especially clothing / shoes / accessories and entertainment).

STARTING AN ECONOMIC ACTIVITY

You need not be residents to start a business in Brazil: simply present a copy of your passport translated by a sworn translator and the CPF ("Cadastre de pessoas físicas", something similar to the Brazilian tax code). To start an activity is necessary to set up a company, this may be "individual", "Limitada", that in some cases may opt for the statement "simple" and pay a five per cent on revenue, or it may be a " Sociedade Anónima ". This has nothing to anonymous, but it is a real spa. Think twice before opening a small business: according to the Sebrae, the entity that provides assistance to small businesses, must comply with 55 requirements for operation, 41 to function normally and eleven to close. And these are the most "mangy".

How do the Brazilians to defend itself from the bureaucracy? Are they all forced to live side by side with lawyers and accountants?

Before you dive in opening the restaurant, cyber café, and more, find out well, as an accountant, what are the best options. The company "individual" is very dangerous because of the personal assets of each is liable for any debts, which does not happen in the "limitada", where the responsibility of every member is just limited to its shareholding. When picking a company, care should be taken to the social contract, which generally tends to favor the Brazilian partner. One thing that there will never be called at the consulate or local authorities is that, to operate in Brazil, it is possible to use a foreign company (including offshore, to ensure the anonymity of members). You may use a representative office in case of investment operations, or a branch, in the case of direct business to the public. The use of a foreign company will allow you, if you wish not to appear and manage it more easily, especially in case of closure or sale. It is important to point out that the use of the foreign company does not seek to evade taxes, to be paid equally.

To deposit their savings in a bank in Brazil is required to provide proof of "residence" on the spot. However, one must actually be living in Brazil?

This is' another of the "great myths": to say that the non-resident can not have a bank account. The problem is that banks do not like foreigners to open accounts and found numerous difficulties. No, by law and having the requirements, even a tourist can open a bank account in Brazil. Among other things, in the practical guide "Investing in Brazil! What to do and what not to do ...! "Are published regulations that allow it. It can be done in a week and must submit, in addition to the tax code in Brazil, namely the aforementioned cpf, the so-called "proof of residence": this may be a bill for electricity, water or telephone, or in a lease registered . Obviously it will take the copy and the original of the passport and the form of entry and exit. These documents are also required to buy a car and to be its owner. For the purchase of property or shares in a company are sufficient to cpf and passport.

BRAZIL GUIDES THE CHARGE OF THE G20

Brazil takes the lead in emerging countries who are opposed to Western dominance. A road leading to a major redefinition of power relationships in business.
Some say no, sang Vasco Rossi. It was back in 1987, the term globalization meant little or nothing, Italians voted against nuclear power and Brazil came out on his knees from a long military dictatorship. Sixteen years later, in Cancun, Mexico, at the summit of the WTO (World Trade Organization) were to say that no other, countries in the developing world. But they "sang" with the same, indistinguishable determination of the artist from Zocca . If the song of Vasco "there is something wrong with the sky" for the representatives of the Global South (more or less industrialized) spoke at the meeting in early September, the injustices on the ground, where the West wants impose rules of the game and absolutely unfair trade.
Unlike three decades ago, however, when the little ones were completely subject to the superpower Soviet and American, now there is a chance to raise his head, and denounce the abuses, relying on the growing authority of

the emerging powers China, India, South Africa and Brazil. After all, times change: the Italians, aided by the power failure, have become wild fan of nuclear energy, while Brazil's government, ideals and outlook much more promising. Very promising to consecrate him as the leader of G20, the group of twenty developing countries, including (in addition to those already mentioned) is also Nigeria, Indonesia and Turkey, who have opposed to Western dominance, in contrast to Cancun instances more effectively than the U.S. Europe.

"We are the first alliance that has the greatest economic and social legitimacy in the world and a large portion of public opinion is on our side of the planet," said Celso Amorim, Brazilian Minister for Trade. "The G20 represents 51% of humanity, 60% of agricultural markets and 63% of all farmers," echoed President Luis Ignacio Lula da Silva Rio.

This would, in short, at least the third force in world trade after the U.S. and Old World: a formidable war machine. And the bogeyman, Robert Zoellick, U.S. representative for foreign trade, is represented just by Brazil in Miami in November, Moose strongly oppose the free trade area covering the Americas (from Alaska glaciers to those of Tierra del Fuego) very strongly desired by America.

Lula, who has repeatedly stressed the importance of Mercosur, in fact, prefer a multilateral system, in order to avoid the social and economic disaster in Mexico caused by NAFTA, the agreement on trade liberalization in Central America. For its part, Amorim, very wisely, has repeatedly cooled the enthusiasm of the post-Cancun, saying that "the real victory is that the G20 proposal on agriculture has been legitimized and form the basis from which to start in Geneva." The real failure of the last WTO summit, in fact, lies not in the rejection of the "Singapore issues", the package for the liberalization of investment on which you are permanently stalled negotiations, but in the obtuse defense by Europe and by U.S. of protectionism in agriculture.

The billion dollar subsidies granted by the White House to American producers of cotton "dope" the formation of world prices, as well as the huge surpluses of food spilled the undertakings on the squares of the Old Continent of Africa: it is these distortions that the G20, joined by Cairns (the association of the world's largest agricultural producers) reported in Cancun, calling for a strong liberalization. Sure, the road ahead is still long, it was not for the fact that the same G20, internally, has strong contradictions. The most progressive currents will become confident in the government led by the Brazilian Workers Party, but not so with the Indian government, fundamentalist and neo-liberal, and with the Chinese, and now close to the authoritarian logic of the Western market.

The real challenge to Lula and the great leader of the Third World will make a general agreement on drastic reduction of subsidies to agriculture in the northern hemisphere in broad agreement that protects even the small farmers, mainly engaged in production for a the domestic market. Brazil, for example, experienced a strong internal contradiction: it is the fourth largest food exporter in the world, but 44 million Brazilians go hungry every day. Again: the G20 might develop a joint program involving industry and services, working as a driving force for cooperation between countries of the South, extending beyond trade to encompass coordination at the level of investment, movement of capital and the social and environmental policies.

The support of civil society in Western Europe (New York Times prophesied at the beginning of the year), the Netherlands will not rebels, as well as by the civil society itself, there will be criticism: Lula at the end of September given the green light to the use of genetically modified soy in the state of Rio Grande do Sul, should know. The road, in short, will be a long, hard and full of pitfalls, but it could lead to a major redefinition of power relationships in business. And, consequently, a more equitable distribution of income worldwide.

THE NEW ARAB BRAZILIAN ...!

The discovery of huge oil field put brazil at the same level of in terms of reserves.

In fact, the bombshell was announced by Petrobras (the news, shares in the Brazilian São Paulo Stock Exchange have surged by more than 15 per cent) after the discovery of the impressive field of Tupi.

A huge oil wealth buried under a thick layer of salt, a country that is transformed into "energy giant" and a president who promises to create a second oil company that devotes its income to social programs. It might seem a literary invention of Jorge Amado, instead it is the political and economic news coming from Brazil in recent weeks.

So Brazil is discovering huge deposits of oil. Are so important that could lead the country the fifth largest reserves in the world and to slide into the background biofuels that only up to a couple of years ago were a priority for the national energy policy.

Thus was born the Saudi Brazil, a major new oil power so that President Lula, who spoke to the nation, the results of oil is so important insights as to represent "a new day of national independence" where it will be the State control these resources. Two years ago the Brazilian sea does not cease to reveal surprises. To the south of the country, under a thick layer of salt that at some point reaches 2,000 meters and 7,000 meters deep under the ocean, in an area of 800 square kilometers off the coast of the states of Espírito Santo and Santa Catarina, there are layers immense. So great that it multiplies up to seven times the reserves in Brazil, passing from 14 to over 90 billion barrels of transforming the country into a world-class oil power, perhaps the fifth for reserves after Saudi Arabia, Iran, Iraq and Kuwait, and levels comparable to the UAE, Russia and Venezuela.

It is a discovery that is so important to completely change the future not only the country's energy, awaken appetites and dangers, but most of all hope. So yesterday, Monday, President Lula spoke of the opening dance, which should lead rapidly to a law that the intention of the State Government gives full control over the oil and redistributes the enormous wealth coming from all states of the country to ensure that oil is "a grace of god that improves the lives of all Brazilians invested the proceeds in three main axes, education, science and technology, as well as in the fight to eradicate poverty". Even for the president, "the oil may represent a new industrial revolution where Brazil wants to export crude oil but not turn into one of the largest petrochemical powers on the planet." A dawn of a new day for Brazil for a president who throws oil on the plate of the campaign to designate who will succeed him. Lula wants to be clear that only the continuity of the government of the PT (Workers Party) that a white woman, Dilma Rousseff, can ensure real progress against the redistributive many vampires. These include the governors of the states off of which the oil is found, which does not agree to share the wealth and those that the president has called "the worshipers of the god of the market," terrified by the fact that oil can be used to benefit of all Brazilians.

Petrobras has acquired the most advanced technology on the planet. This year he has invested a billion dollars, production began in March 2009 and amounts to 100 thousand barrels per day and 3.5 million cubic meters of gas. Since 2017, the production increase. Meanwhile, nearly completed the construction of a huge submersible platform, called P-51, equipped for 200 people, a weight of 48 thousand tons and a capacity for extraction of a scheme will be 180 thousand barrels of oil a day.

So much energy wealth can project Brazil Olympus large producing countries, but can also lead to "Dutch curse" or the nemesis who punishes the owners of large natural resources. That's why Lula has announced a "revision" of the model of oil exploration in Brazil. It is the creation of a new oil company (who will support Petrobras) with a very specific mission: to support social programs. The company is characterized by a greater state presence in the management of newly discovered deposits.

In fact the area explored is only a small part of the coastline that stretches for 800 km from the state of Espirito Santo to that of Santa Caterina, potentially rich in oil and gas. Brazil is currently in 17th place only between countries with oil reserves but this discovery puts him in 8th place at least equal to Saudi Arabia and Venezuela, but the potential reserves could be much higher if you decide to explore the whole area.

Oil is placed at great depth (the Tupi field lies under 2,100 meters of water, more than 3000 meters of sand and rocks, and another 2000 meters of a hard layer of salt), but with modern technology is not a problem pull together gas.

E 'therefore conceivable that Brazil, as well as being the largest producer of biofuels, will become between 3-4 years (when the plants are in operation) also one of the leading world exporters of oil. Considering that Brazil is very rich of all other raw materials (iron, uranium, coal, aluminum, soybean, wheat, coffee, sugar etc ...) and given the growing strategic importance, economic status and political commodity, as indeed has ironically The Economist reported, "Perhaps God is Brazilian? ...)

SOCIAL PROJECT

The explanation of the project was entrusted to Aloisio Mercadante, a senator of the PT (the Workers' Party, the same as Lula): "We are inspired by the model adopted in Norway, where he was created a fund of 400 billion dollars, with a distributive philosophy also aims to ensure that future generations of the proceeds of oil wealth. In order to avoid being reduced as Saudi Arabia, Iran and Iraq, where industrialization is not adequate. "

Fears of a populist management is pragmatic, however, been allayed by the Minister of Mines and Energy, Edison Lobao, "The new law Lula will not affect the interests of foreign companies operating in the existing fields."

Brazil is the 3rd as the growth of millionaires in the world. In 2007, according to a study released by Capgemini and Merrill Lynch, Brazil had a growth of 19.1% of the amount of people with liquid assets over U.S. $ 1 million in the previous year. The number of millionaires in the country has increased from 120,000 to 143,000.

According to this study, India ranks first place with a growth of 22.7%, China is in second place with a growth of 20.3%. Russia, however (the last representatives of the BRIC format precisely from Brazil, Russia, India and China) is at 10th place with an increase of 14.4%.

Worldwide growth in the number of millionaires in 2007 than in 2006 was 6%.

The middle class is growing in Brazil
As we have already 'seen, Brazil is reducing the level of inequality in wealth distribution, reaching in 2007 the highest percentage in the history of the population of Class C (the middle class in Brazil, according to a classification in 5 classes AE).

The research carried out by the FGV shows the percentage of poverty in the country has declined from 19.6% in 2006 to 18% in 2007 with 1.5 million people left the poverty line just reaching the middle class. The new C-class reaches the figure of 47.06% of the population in 2007. The middle class is the one band that runs from 1064 to 4591 reais as family income.

Despite the ongoing crisis in the world as Brazil continues to grow.

The scale of tourism in Brazil is negative in the first eight months of 2008
According to data from Banco Central (BC) in the first eight months of 2008

were U.S. $ 7.85 billion already spent by tourists in Brazil and abroad. This amount represents an increase of 57.5% over 2007.

But even the spending of inbound tourism in Brazil has set a record with U.S. $ 3.86 billion in the first 8 months with an increase of 18.46% compared to 2007. This finding is significant because it shows how the inbound tourism in Brazil is growing well above the world average of 7%.

Despite this, the Brazilian trade balance in tourism is negative, but in reality this figure is very positive as it demonstrates the increased power of the income of the Brazilian population, which now travels abroad and spends far more than incoming tourists in Brazil can do.

Foreign direct investment record in Brazil in the first 8 months of 2008
In the first 8 months already have been in Brazil U.S. $ 24.575 billion of foreign direct investment (FDI). The ongoing global financial crisis does not seem to now have affected Brazil.

Unemployment rate falls again in Brazil
In August 2008 the unemployment rate in Brazil fell to 7.6% according to the Brazilian Institute of Geography and Statistics. The index is better than July 2008 (8.1%) and especially in relation to August 2007 when the unemployment rate was 9.5%.

BRAZILIAN ECONOMY GROWS 5.4% IN 2007
The gross domestic product (GDP) and grew by 5.4% in 2007 worth 2.6 trillion reais (about 1,000 billion euro), driven by investment growth (+13.4%) who had the higher rate of development from 1996.L 'industry has grown by 4.9%, the services sector by 4.7%. Another major factor in development in 2007 was the growth in domestic consumption of resident households (+6.5%).

Exports rose by 6.6%, however, held back by the strong appreciation of the real hand that pushed imports (+20.7%).

GDP growth for 2008 was around 5%.

PROFITABILITY OF BRAZILIAN INDUSTRIES IS MORE THAN THE U.S. ONE.
In 2007 the return on liquid assets of industries traded on the Brazilian stock exchange in Sao Paulo has reached 16.02% and exceeded the profitability of

U.S. industries still at 14.6%

BRAZIL NEED TO 27.2 MILLION HOMES BY 2020

To meet the growing demand for housing according to a study prepared by the civil union of the construction industry of São Paulo (SP SINDUSCON) is necessary to increase the pace of civil construction. Currently being built in Brazil, 1.6 million homes per year. You will then need to be increased to at least 2 million years of housing to meet the needs of the population.

The study confirms the growing trend of development in Brazil and estimated a growth cycle expected for at least the next decade.

MINIMUM WAGE RISES TO 412 REAIS IN MARCH 2007

The growth is 8.52% compared to previous Brazilian minimum wage (380 reais). Today in 2010 it is growing still coming to 485 reais.

BRAZIL IS THE BEST EMERGING MARKET OF THE WORLD ACCORDING TO CITIBANK

The recent good performance of the Brazilian stock market has elevated the weight of the country in the MSCI emerging markets at Morgan Stanley, to 14.95% for the first time surpassing China and South Korea Dennios According to Geoffrey, an analyst at Citibank, "Brazil is now the biggest emerging market equity and one-tenth of the world." Among the industries Brazil's Petrobras is the largest emerging company in the world in terms of capitalization, in second place are the Russian Gazprom and the third largest of a new industry in Brazil, is worth it.

BRAZIL IS A CREDITOR COUNTRY FOR THE FIRST TIME IN ITS HISTORY

Brazil has ceased to be a debtor country abroad and has become in January 2008 for the first time a creditor nation. Brazilian assets abroad exceeded the debt. According to the Central Bank, the unprecedented increase in international reserves in recent months and the advance payment of foreign debt have enabled Brazil to become for the first time in its history a creditor nation.

The effect of this new situation has helped Brazil to achieve the AAA rating in 2009, which is the most industrialized economies in terms of reliability of its economic system.

BRAZIL TO 6th PLACE AMONG THE BEST COUNTRIES FOR FOREIGN INVESTMENT

In 2007, Brazil has won a position in the ranking drawn up by AT Kearney's index of confidence for Foreign Direct Investment 2007, published annually by the prestigious U.S. consulting firm.

China leads the standings, followed by India, USA, Great Britain, Hong Kong, Brazil. Russia, which along with China and India and Brazil form the BRIC is in 9th place.

Brazil is the 5th best country in the world where to invest according to a study made public Oct. 4 UN in Geneva. According to the study of international corporate investment will grow over the next three years. Brazil in the ranking order is preceded by China, India, United States, and Russia. Among European countries only the United Kingdom and Poland are among the top 10 places.

The industrial production increased by 1 .3% in August compared to July and 6.6% since August 2006 and scored it the 14th consecutive rise. Business confidence in Brazil has reached a score of 123.7 in July marking the historical record since 1995 when the trust was measured for the first time. The index advanced 2.9% from June and 15.8% compared to July 2006.

Fiat strong growth in Brazil. The budget for the third quarter of 2007 in Brazil for the Fiat group shows an increase of 30% at 143 000 units, close to the performance level achieved in Italy (155 thousand, an increase of 7%) but with a much higher profitability.

The unemployment rate in July decreased 9.7% compared to 10.1% in June. The number of employed persons is 20.79 million with an increase of 3.2% over the same period last year. The average wage of the worker is Reais 1119.20 per month with an increase of 2.7% compared to July last year. Over 105 million Brazilians have a mobile phone. In the first five months of 2007 there were 5,179,000 new members, an increase of 5.18% over the first five months of 2006   General Electric (GE) is optimistic the housing market in Brazil and Mexico:

"We are increasing the exposure of our property investment in Mexico and we Geraci entering the Brazilian market, we consider Brazil as the future of Mexico," said Joseph Parsons, president of GE Real Estate. "The country is stabilizing, the government is pro-active and well prepared for investment, has great natural resources, has a growing middle class and a very positive dynamic"

Great opportunity for growth in real estate credit

Industry Minister Miguel Jorge provides funding for the purchase of property must achieve in the next year totaling at least 10% of GDP. Brazil currently reaches only 2% of GDP due to a historical situation that because of high interest rates and economic instability has slowed the housing market. In Europe the average secured credit reaches 20% of GDP. Brazil is the 9th place among the world's most attractive countries for investment according to a study released in June 2007 by Ernst & Young. China is firmly at the top while among the European countries only Germany stands in 4th place.

Citigroup sees the Bovespa at 70,000 points within a year. The influential financial group said that Brazil is its greatest challenge in Latin America and that he had never seen in the last 15 years so much optimism about Brazil as now. "Rarely have we seen so much solid economic prospects." The Energies Silf Portuguese company based in Fortaleza provides for investments of 3.9 billion dollars in wind energy in the coming years. The wind turbines will be installed in Ceara and the first implementation is already underway in the area of Aquiraz (Fortaleza) and produce only 20% of the energy needed for the entire state of Ceara.

Brazil will resume construction of Angra 3, the third nuclear power plant in the country according to a plan that aims to build seven nuclear power stations in coming decades.

Stock Exchange

The Bovespa update the historical record and breaks through the wall of 51,000 points.

Indicators

The sale of new cars registered in the first 4 months of 2007 increased by 22.6% over the first four months of 2006.

Fiat has saturated the capacity of its plant in Betim (Minas Gerais), which is currently the largest Fiat plant in the world and has assumed additional 1200 workers ... while we ... For now, the excess demand is offset by the importation of car from the factory in Cordoba (Argentina) but the house automibilistica Turin is considering opening a new establishment in the

territory to meet the strong future demand for cars in Brazil. The trade balance recorded in April, the best result this year with a surplus of U.S. $ 4.203 billion. The forecast for 2007 is a positive balance of U.S. $ 40 billion ... while we maneuvers and maneuver for ...
Industrial production in March 2007 marked an increase of 1, 2% on February 2007 and 3.9% in March 2006.

National Economy
"The world will be converted to bio-fuel" these are the words of President Luiz Inacio Lula da Silva at the Expo Zebu 2007, "the process is irreversible, and when that happens no one can compete with Brazil." Since 1 May speech of Lula "I have reason to be optimistic. Our expectation is that, with economic growth, and the numbers indicate that the economy will continue to grow in an increasingly robust in the coming years, and the acceleration of the implementation of the program (CAP) and even with the exemption of tax that we did on civil and building material for their civil construction, there have tremendous potential to generate jobs. "
Brazil has terminated earlier debts to the IMF (and PIIGS while Greece, Portugal, Italy, Ireland and Spain ...) and has been very successful in terms of trade balance and holds a record level of foreign reserves. It is no longer so vulnerable to changes in the flow of foreign investment.
IMPLICATIONS: The increased level of confidence will greatly increase the flow of foreign investment to the country. Brazil will pay less in interest on its debt. Another likely consequence is the progressive enhancement of the Real, however, which could bring negative effects on exports. At this point it is likely that the central bank will lower the interest rate SELICE (currently 12.50%) to curb the power of the Real, a situation that will generate more positive effects on the Brazilian.

RIO IS! BRAZIL AT THE OLYMPIC GAMES OF 2016

Rio de Janeiro was chosen by the IOC to host the 2016 Olympics. "We are the only ones among the ten largest economies in the world, had never hosted an Olympics," said President Lula. "For others it was simply more of an Olympiad, will be an opportunity for us unparalleled (...). This application is not only ours, but of all South America A continent that has never hosted the Olympic Games. It's time to correct this mistake. A great victory for Lula, then, for all over Brazil and throughout South America.

The project presented by Rio was the most expensive among the four finalists. The estimated expenditure is 14.42 billion dollars, compared to 4.82 for Chicago, 6.13 in Madrid and 6.8 in Tokyo.

19 spaces will be exploited erected at the Pan-American in 2007, and 11 more will be built from scratch.

Do not forget that Brazil is sworn in, only two years before the Olympic competition, including the World Cup of Football (Brazil 2014). In short, the country overwhelmingly skip the headlines. It's not just sports, international reach, prestige: it is an impressive round of money, jobs, tourists, a really great challenge that involves numerous risks, first and foremost the safety (of the athletes and guests) and procurement millionaires (we Italians know something, we are masters of illicit enrichment). It is a great, great success it deserves to be celebrated. Caipirinha for everyone!

SHANGHAI EXPO 2010: BRAZIL PAVILION

There are also designs for two Brazilian cities, among the 48 selected worldwide area devoted to the Expo 2010 Shanghai Urban Best Practices (GFP): This is Sao Paulo and Porto Alegre. With 70 million visitors expected for the period of its duration (six months from May to November 2010), the Shanghai World Expo promises to be the largest exhibition of the history of nations.

St. Paul, with the Clean Cities project, was ranked fourth. In addition to the economic, St. Paul shows the various attractions that represent the culture and the development of the city, with a focus on urban renewal and the fight against pollution.

Porto Alegre, capital of Rio Grande do Sul, instead presenting an innovative development project entitled "Supportive Local Government (Local Governance Solidaria - PGSL), which focuses on flexibility to ensure wide participation and facilitate the formation of cooperation networks and partnerships effective. At the base of the PGSL, the experience of participatory democracy in Porto Alegre, the result of historical experiences of the EU and the strength of the longer popular participation in the distribution of public resources - the Participatory Budget.

With the theme of vibrant cities, the Brazilian Pavilion for Expo Shanghai 2010 will present the human and cultural diversity of Brazilian cities, the dynamism of its large cities and its economy booming, highlighting the high-tech industries and major progress the country in the field of sustainability and social inclusion and politics.

The pavilion will also host a number of artistic, cultural and tourism, thematic discussions, business meetings and events dedicated to gastronomy, and a large exposure to ethnic, cultural and landscape of Brazil through photos, videos, music, entertainment and food. The narrative is divided into three thematic areas: sustainable development, diversity / global city, popular participation and social inclusion.

Brazil will also promote seminars and discussions with other countries on issues such as renewable energy, the policies of water management and technological innovation. For the larger forum of discussion of the event, the country will lead to the conclusions of the 5th World Urban Forum, held in March 2010 in Rio de Janeiro, and the 15th Conference of the Parties of the United Nations on Climate Change (COP 15), which is held in December in Copenhagen.

THE FRUIT OF BRAZIL

One of the products in Brazil is very rich it is the fruit. In most cases they are never seen fruit on our tables. The variety of fruit in Brazil is unusually high and excellent quality: pineapple, banana, cashew, passion fruit, papayas, melons, grapes, apples, walnuts. The Amazon provides many types of tropical fruits such as Bacuri, cupuassu, jenipapo, mangaba, tapereba. The most famous are Carambola, guarana, guava, passion fruit, Jacca. Currently, Brazil is one of the top three global giants in the production of fruit, with an annual volume of 41 million tonnes. Due to its climatic conditions, the extension of its territory, geographical position and the nature of the soil, Brazil can produce various types of fruit: tropical, subtropical and temperate areas of the typical.

IBRAF operates in Brazil (Brazilian Fruit Institute), founded in 1990 by major industry players. This is a non-profit organization created to carry out market research, promote training and the advanced technology in the field and outline the fruit industry guidelines. To give impetus to exports of fresh and processed fruits from Brazil, IBRAF, in collaboration with other organizations and associations, has launched an initiative called "Brazilian Fruit Project". This promotion program affects the following product types: lime, apple, mango, melon, papaya, grapes, pineapple, bananas, oranges, tangerines, peaches, persimmons, figs, strawberries and watermelons for fruit to be eaten fresh. Pulp, juice, peanut, coconut water and more, with respect to the converted. From 1998 to 2006, exports of fruits from Brazil have increased exponentially by 170% in volume terms (from about 297,000 tons to over 802,000 tons) and 296% in value terms (about $ 120 million to over 472 million dollars). This enabled the Brazilian trade balance of fruit and vegetables (see table below) to increase its focus - after several years (1994 - 1998) budget person - up to a maximum of $ 315 million in assets in 2005 (292 million dollars in 2006).

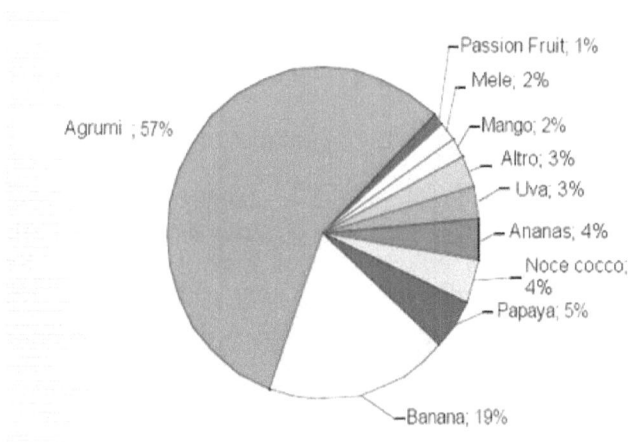

T
HE MIRACULOUS FRUIT: ACEROLA
The Acerola (Malpighia glabra) is an incredible result of which we in the West even heard of. And 'the fruit that contains more vitamin C in the world (almost 30 times more of the orange), also contains antioxidants, anti-free radicals, very good to combat this form of influenza in those who smoke to help the absorption of iron, anti viral , stimulates the immune system.

It 's a miracle plant that grows wild in Central and South America, especially Brazil and Puerto Rico.

E 'especially useful for its high content of vitamin C (100 gr. Acerola give about 1,000 to 2,000 mg. Vitamin C) and because it can combat free radicals, for colds, flu, lung problems, colds , bronchitis, sinusitis, and all the problems affecting the respiratory system, useful for liver problems, and useful in viral infections in viral hepatitis in the chicken pox, polio and also has a high antioxidant activity, which is probably due to its high content of vitamin C. The use of the fruits is used in diarrhea (Always consult your doctor).

Vitamin C is not synthesized by the body and should therefore be taken as a supplement, Vitamin C is essential for the formation of collagen, the synthesis of hormones, tissue regeneration, because of its antioxidant action is helpful for the immune system. It is a plant together with Rosehip essential for its high content of Vitamin C for smokers, as each cigarette burns significant amounts of Vitamin C.

Vitamin C stimulates the synthesis of folic acid to effect tissue regeneration, prevents the formation of nitrosamines (carcinogenic), enhances iron absorption.

Guaranà

Guaranà (Paullinia cupana Kunth) is a climber, evergreen, native to the Amazon rainforest. In the wild can grow up to twelve meters in height, may be lean on the trees of the forest (do not create any damage to another plant), and remain upright without support. When, however, is grown for industrial use, is required in the form of tree or shrub, no higher than two to three feet, to facilitate the collection of his precious seed. Guaranà has a long history. It was a sacred plant for many tribes of Indians. Because of her "strange" result, around this small plant, which would perhaps otherwise go unnoticed, were born many legends and myths.

There are legends in a very remote time, had as its protagonist a girl that looks and gentle soul, her name was Cereaporanga and was protected by the goddess of beauty and life. Cereaporanga One day she met a brave warrior of an enemy tribe and fell in love with him. Their love would overcome everything, but the two lovers would never be able to stop the hatred that existed for years between the two tribes, so they decided to elope to be happy. During the journey she meets an injured anaconda and, despite the danger, her sweet heart led her to help her, treated her with all her affection, but she did not know that this gesture would have been fatal.

Because of this "rest", the warriors of his tribe came more and more, then, conscious of being chased and certain that his man was captured and killed, made a covenant of love and death, he asked the big snake string, with all his might, in their last embrace.

The Indians, seeing the two lovers in their latest action, despair over the death of their protection. They asked for help once the goddess of beauty and life that at least the spirit of the woman does not abandon them, so the goddess, touched by the gesture of Cereaporanga, gave birth from his eyes a plant whose fruits appear, at the opening, two beautiful eyes blacks , just as those of the most beautiful girl.

Guaranà has been considered by the Indians as the elixir of life, its importance was high in all the various tribes, as it provided them with food and the means to cure disease, prepare and support the body. Its use was primarily centered on the effect of tonic-stimulant, and was then used to increase physical endurance, hunting, etc.. Many tribes of Indians, however, went beyond this apparent effect, and use Guaranà for combat diarrhea, relieve menstrual pain, for diseases that weakened - and to be able to see / understand things around us; surely a purpose connected with the fact that the plant itself has eyes to see.

They were used only seeds, and each tribe had its own system to prepare them. But, in general, Brazilian Indians, they all tend to the same preparation: picking the grapes, choosing the fruits when they are semi-open, which were placed in containers filled with cold water to extract the skin coloring, and, after cleaning, are roasted over a low heat on the same day of collection, after which they are crushed.

Reduced seed powder, add a bit of water, continuing to crush them to form a smooth paste. To this paste you give them a form of stick and goes in the sun after the fumigation is made of resinous wood fire. This dough is then grated at the time of need.

In preparations of Venezuela, however, the seeds are stripped from the shells crushed in hot water, supplemented with cassava flour, left to ferment for a time and mixed with boiling water until a paste that is dried and fumigated. Guaranà is widely used in South America for the preparation of a famous soft drink, lightly fizzy, called just "Guaranà", similar in appearance and taste the different types of cola-based drinks, which has a subtle effect of stimulating and a sweet taste. For its medicinal use is to be found in tablets, sticks or, better yet, in the dust. Recently, the European market, are also commercially candy and chocolates made with guaranà.

Chemical composition (in dry seeds)
Vegetable fiber 49%
Starch 9%
Water 7 / 8%
Pectin, dextrin, minerals, malic acid, 7 / 8%
* 5% tannic acid
Guaranina (caffeine) 4 / 5%
Fixed oil 2 / 3%
Acid pyro-guarana 2%
1% glucose
0.06% saponin
* Guaranatina guaranatannico or acid, similar to the Kolatina Kola nut

Theobromine is present in the flowers, leaves and bark, but no seeds

Therapeutic properties
The properties of Guaranà are innumerable, widely tested, documented and, depending on the subject, an effect prevails over another. However, thanks to its high content of natural active ingredients is manifested by a sense of immediate well-being, readily identifiable, the temperature of the body reaches an ideal level and remains in its normal state.
It is a stimulant effective in all states of nervous depression, drowsiness, adynamia consecutive infections, malaria, aids digestion and is easier in those ipopeptici fact, winning it with the headache consecutive meals of

persons with slow digestion, so it is also stomachic .

Vince often habitual constipation, promoting the contraction of the muscle fibers of the intestinal walls, helps with the bloating. Excites the nerve centers on the one hand, and especially the brain, which makes it easier and more intense activity and on the other side of the circulatory function, strengthening the cardiac contraction, increasing the pressure endovasale.

According to scientific research, guarana has properties antianemic, antineuralgic, stimulant, analgesic, aphrodisiac, anti-diarrhea and constipation at the same time free from (given that fights infection of microbes that attack the gastrointestinal system, is a large intestinal disinfectant). This seed is also a powerful diuretic and diaphoretic, and helps eliminate excess fluids in the body, moreover, reduces the stimulus of hunger, so it is useful in slimming diets.

It is also an excellent preventive against the evils of old age is an excellent tonic for the elderly.

Aquarela

Numa folha qualquer eu desenho um sol amarelo
E com cinco ou seis retas é fácil fazer um castelo.
Corro o lápis em torno da mão e me dou uma luva,
E se faço chover, com dois riscos tenho um guarda-chuva.

Se um pinguinho de tinta cai num pedacinho azul do papel,
Num instante imagino uma linda gaivota a voar no céu.
Vai voando, contornando a imensa curva Norte e Sul,
Vou com ela, viajando, Havaí, Pequim ou Istambul.
Pinto um barco a vela branco, navegando, é tanto céu e mar num
beijo azul.

Entre as nuvens vem surgindo um lindo avião rosa e grená.
Tudo em volta colorindo, com suas luzes a piscar.
Basta imaginar e ele está partindo, sereno, indo,
E se a gente quiser ele vai pousar.

Numa folha qualquer eu desenho um navio de partida
Com alguns bons amigos bebendo de bem com a vida.
De uma América a outra consigo passar num segundo,
Giro um simples compasso e num círculo eu faço o mundo.

Um menino caminha e caminhando chega no muro
E ali logo em frente, a esperar pela gente, o futuro está.
E o futuro é uma astronave que tentamos pilotar,
Não tem tempo nem piedade, nem tem hora de chegar.
Sem pedir licença muda nossa vida, depois convida a rir ou chorar.

Nessa estrada não nos cabe conhecer ou ver o que virá.
O fim dela ninguém sabe bem ao certo onde vai dar.
Vamos todos numa linda passarela.
De uma aquarela que um dia, enfim, descolorirá.
Numa folha qualquer eu desenho um sol amarelo (que descolorirá).
E com cinco ou seis retas é fácil fazer um castelo (que descolorirá).
Giro um simples compasso e num círculo eu faço o mundo (que descolorirá).

Toquinho E Vinicius De Moraes

Watercolor

On a sheet of paper you see the sun and yellow
but if it rains two pen marks give you an umbrella
the trees are nothing but bottles of wine shot
if you put the two types below will be drunk
grass, and always green and if you see a distant point
it can be or the God or a seagull that runs away.
To fly to the sea and the sea and all blue
and a ship to sail a sailboat and no more
but under water the fish know where to go
where it seems not where you want it
and the sky is watching and the sky is always blue
There is a plane up there at the top and the plane goes down '
there is who greets him on the ground with his hand
go slowly out of a bar who knows where it goes.
On a sheet of paper you see people traveling in a train
are three good friends who travel and speak up
It is a joke from another America takes a second
just make a nice circle and here you have the whole world
a guy walks walks coming to a wall
closes his eyes for a moment and before you see the future already is.
And the future is spaceship that has no time or mercy
Mars goes where it wants to know nothing ever gonna stop
if we encounter no noise
does not ask for love and does not give, so let's go on
work in the city that we have a little fear
but the fear will pass we are all at stake
beauty in a watercolor that discolors
that fade.

On a sheet of paper
you see the sun and yellow but fade
but if it rains two pen marks
give you an umbrella that discolors
just make a nice circle and here
you have the whole world fade.

Toquinho E Vinicius De Moraes

CONTACT:

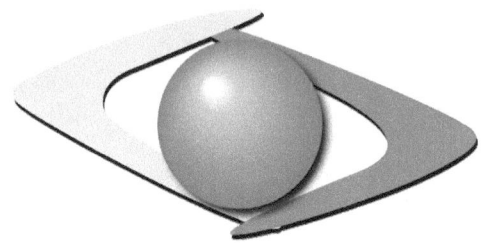

www.brazilrealproperty.com

info@brazilrealproperty.com

brazilrealproperty

MSN: msn@brazilrealproperty.com

NOTES

LIBRI CONSIGLIATI

Anthony Robbins

Awaken the Giant Within : How to Take Immediate Control of Your Mental, Emotional, Physical and Financial Destiny!

Robert T. Kiyosaki

Rich Dad Poor Dad

Robert T. Kiyosaki

Conspiracy of the Rich

Eugenio Benetazzo

Best Before - Preparati al Peggio!

Eugenio Benetazzo

Duri e Puri

Silvano Agosti

Lettere dalla Kirghisia

DELLO STESSO AUTORE

In questo pratico e veloce libro sono raccolti, andando direttamente al nocciolo di ogni situazione e soprattutto senza filtri, dieci anni di diretta esperienza in Brasile in materia di investimenti.

INVESTIRE IN BRASILE COSA FARE E COSA NON... FARE!

Vi permetterà di partire già con un bagaglio di esperienza in materia di investimenti immobiliari e di non cadere nella miriade di "trucchetti" che inevitabilmente incontrerete nel paese del "samba" venendo a conoscenza delle CRUDE VERITA'!

Non permettete che il Vostro Paradiso si trasformi nel Vostro Inferno...
A voi la scelta!
Abraço

INVESTIRE IN BRASILE

Brazil Real Property

INVESTIRE IN BRASILE

ORDEM E PROGRESSO

COSA FARE E COSA NON... FARE!

In this practical guide
have been collected the
results of a ten years
experience in terms of
investments that Brazil
Real Property has
matured in Brazil, deeply
analyzing every single
situation.

INVESTING IN BRAZIL
WHAT TO DO AND
WHAT... NOT TO DO!

It will let you get started
having already a
considerable experience of real estate
investments so that you won't be victim of
the myriad of "tricks" that you will
inevitably run into, being aware of the
rough truth.

Don't let your Paradise turn into your Hell...
You can choose!

Editor: Brazil Real Property
2008 Brazil Real Property Standard
Copyright License
New Edition 2010
www.brazilrealproperty.com

INVESTING IN BRAZIL

Brazil Real Property

INVESTING IN BRAZIL

ORDEM E PROGRESSO

WHAT TO DO AND
WHAT... NOT TO DO!

En este práctico y cómodo libro se recogen rápidamente, yendo directamente al núcleo de la situación y sobre todo sin filtros, diez años de experiencia directa de Inversión en de Bienes e Inmuebles en Brasil.

**INVERSIONES EN BRASIL
QUE HACER Y QUE... NO HACER!**

Iniciemos con nuestra amplia experiencia en inversiones inmobiliarias y no caigamos en la miríada de "trucos" que inevitablemente se encontrarán en el "país de la samba", seamos conscientes de la cruda realidad. No deje que su Paraíso se convierta en tu Infierno ...
La elección es suya!

www.brazilrealproperty.com

ISBN 978-1-4461-6805-9

INVERSIONES EN BRASIL

Brazil Real Property

INVERSIONES
EN BRASIL

ORDEM E PROGRESSO

QUE HACER Y
QUE
... NO HACER!

ISBN 978-1-4452-0099-5

141

VIVIR DE
RENTA A
40 AÑOS

EN

BRAZIL

La globalización que prometió, después del
derrumbamiento de la Unión Soviética y el consiguiente
fin de la guerra fría, un período de paz augusto, no ha
faltado de revelar el engaño español; y el mundo vuelve
a ser para pocas potencias élite el tablero de juegos
de estrategia geopolítica cada vez más penetrante;
nosotros los pocos sacrificales a menudo ignoros del
juego.

En este escenario en rápido cambio, es más que nunca
fundamental entender dónde el mundo está yendo... o
mejor ¡DÓNDE, EN EL MUNDO ES MEJOR IR!

Con este nuevo trabajo editorial queremos consolidar la
opinión, avalorada por experiencias personales, que
Brazil todavía está entre los pocos países en
crecimiento al mundo y se entrebebe una de las últimas
fronteras dónde construir un futuro posible.

[texto ilegible] aquí

[texto ilegible] de la gente a la libre
[texto ilegible] a 40 días de sol al año, ¿ a tí etcétera y las
[texto ilegible] que se viven aquí.

VIVIR DE RENTA EN BRAZIL A 40 AÑOS"

Con esta nueva guía práctica queremos compartir este
lugar mágico junto a vosotros.
¡El punto de salto!

ISBN 978-1-4461-2419-2
90000

VIVIR DE RENTA A 40 AÑOS EN BRAZIL

BRAZIL REAL PROPERTY

143

www.ingramcontent.com/pod-product-compliance
Lightning Source LLC
Chambersburg PA
CBHW021952170526
45157CB00003B/961